PARIS

A GUIDE
TO HOTELS
OF CHARM
INCLUDING OUTLYING DISTRICTS

© Rivages, 1991
27 rue de Fleurus - 75006 Paris
10 rue Fortia - 13001 Marseille

Distributed in the English speaking world by
Roger Lascelles
47 York Road, Brentford TW8 0QP, Middlesex
England
Tel 081-847 0935

PARIS

A GUIDE TO HOTELS OF CHARM

INCLUDING OUTLYING DISTRICTS

Guide written by
Catherine Nuridsany and Laurence Bonnet

Translated
by Agathe Moitessier

Photographs by
Véronique Pettit De Andreis
and Catherine Nuridsany

Rivages

Photographs :

13 : Patrice Desphelippon - 20 : Philippe Gabel - 25 : M. Silve -
26 : Dany Arrault - 33 : Sylvie Vernichon - 43 : Laurent Caro - 55 :
Azad - 61 : Alexandre Bailhache - 74 : Michel Urtado - 91 : Pascal
Bouclier - 111 : Leader Communication - 138 : Antoine Labrado -
15, 22, 57, 65, 133 : DR - 60, 76, 87 : Eliophot, Aix-en-Provence.

Foreword

People often ask us : "What do you mean by charm when you speak of a hotel ?" The best answer was provided by a reader : "A hotel where you feel at ease the minute you are inside." This is true : whatever the style of the place, the atmosphere is a criterion on which we always agree...

Style evolves in the Parisian hotel business. And for the best. When hotels are renovated, it is done with care and a sense for quality, it is the work of professionals. Even in 2-star establishments. The artful arrangement allowing to fit a bathroom in the smallest nook or cranny and the sweet thrift-shop bric-à-brac was replaced in new hotels of charm by an intelligent disposition pertaining a "touch of class" to the place : space, subtle colours, beautiful materials (wood, cut glass, mosaics), furniture with sharp lines and a diffuse lighting which suffuses this pure refinement.

And when the decoration shows more originality, it is done with brilliance : bedrooms different from one another, restored antique furniture...

These are the characteristics of the 23 new addresses we found in Paris. In areas where you don't find many hotels of charm, or others showing how the city centres move : Champs-Elysées, Montparnasse, Bastille (with its new Opera house !)

Then, we also felt that we should enlarge our researches around Paris. We privileged touristic sights calling for an escapade during the weekend : forests, rivers, parks and castles. We were delighted to find out that places looking like old postcards still existed. We chose 23 addresses. This is the new part of this 1991 edition.

Catherine Nuridsany
and Laurence Bonnet

How to use
Paris - A Guide to Hotels of Charm, Including Outlying Districts

Quarter after quarter and for outlying districts, region after region, each address we put in this 1991 edition is presented on one page, with a photograph, informations and a description of its atmosphere.

Completing these detailed descriptions, we highlight the price category, the number of stars and its location with the help of several indexes and maps which you shall find at the end of the book, with, of course, the necessary alphabetical index...

Some of these addresses were recommended by our readers. Your observations and suggestions are always welcome, keep on writing to :

Editions Rivages
Paris - A Guide to Hotels of Charm, Including Outlying Districts
27 rue de Fleurus - 75006 Paris
France

RIVE GAUCHE - LEFT BANK

NOTRE-DAME CATHEDRAL - THE CITE

In France, all the roads start in front of Notre-Dame Cathedral which is the heart of Paris, just as Paris is the heart of France. This is where you begin to discover the Medieval Paris, with the Sainte-Chapelle, the Conciergerie, the charming flower market and a bit further, over the Seine river, the churches of Saint-Séverin and Saint-Julien-le-Pauvre.

ILE SAINT-LOUIS

Between the Cité and the district of the Marais, the "island" is Paris most sophisticaded "village", very famous abroad. You will note the beautiful 17th century architecture in the rue Saint-Louis-en-l'Ile along which you find restaurants, attractive boutiques and famous delicatessens.

QUARTIER LATIN (LATIN QUARTER)

From the Seine river to the Panthéon and from Maubert to Odéon, this Gallo-Roman and Medieval district is not far from the Cité. It was one of the Revolution's active centres and is now the students' quarter, where ideas quickly take hold of the street crowds. Even if boutiques are now more numerous than bookstores, it still has the charm of a youthful and cosmopolitan population. This variegated crowd gives life to the terraces of the cafés on the boulevard Saint-Michel, and fills the neighbouring cinemas.

* ❀ indicates hotels with a garden or a patio.

JARDIN DES PLANTES (BOTANICAL GARDENS)

An animated and simple district where you can stroll endlessly from the Seine river to the Montagne Sainte-Geneviève. It goes from the large tropical greenhouses in the Botanical Gardens to the Arènes de Lutèce, and includes the mosque and the market of the rue Mouffetard, called "la Mouffe".

PARC MONTSOURIS

In the most hidden part of the 14th arrondissement, almost bordering the ring road and not far from the South ring road, this is a quiet district with two very large gardens : the Parc Montsouris and the campus of the Cité Internationale Universitaire. Private houses and blind alleys, listed among the most beautiful in Paris, let you discover the architecture of the 1920s with masters such as Le Corbusier, Sauvage or Lurçat...

MONTPARNASSE

This district, which starts at the Montparnasse railway station goes to Port-Royal and follows the rue de Vaugirard to Denfert-Rochereau, still has the atmosphere of a village ; you will find everywhere artists' studios, private alleys, art deco style buildings and little houses built in the last century. However, it is changing now (Montparnasse Tower and Boffil's buildings). Popular and lively, it is a shopping district with an animated night life : theatres, restaurants, cinemas and cafés are everywhere along the rue de la Gaîté and the boulevard du Montparnasse.

LUXEMBOURG

At the heart of a triangle formed by Saint-Germain-des-Prés, the Latin Quarter and Montparnasse, this district's life beats to the rythm of the student life. Not far from the flower beds "à la française" and the shaded terraces, there is the orchard of the Gardening School and the bee-hives where, during the summer, ladies and gentlemen come to study bee-keeping.

SAINT-GERMAIN-DES-PRES

Marked by the fieverish intellectual and artistic atmosphere of the years following World War II, this village has now lost its fame in favour of Beaubourg and the Bastille district, but it still is animated day and night. An area where publishers, antique dealers and fashion designers have settled and where cafés, restaurants, jazz clubs and night-clubs are countless ; it offers a happy combination of lively activities.

FAUBOURG SAINT-GERMAIN

Already at the end of the 18th century, the aristocracy moved here away from the Marais ; aristocrats crossed the Seine river to build the town houses which you can admire today. Extremely residential, this district shelters ministries and embassies, and behind its high walls, hides convents and private gardens. Two famous museums : Rodin and Orsay. A place renowned for its antique shops and known as the Carré Rive Gauche.

TOUR EIFFEL (EIFFEL TOWER)

Surmounted by the most famous monument in Paris, this is a district enclosed by the large gardens of the Invalides and the Champ de Mars. It has two very different aspects : on one side it is quiet, with little animation and residential, on the other side, animated with a lot of shops. It is more and more appreciated by businessmen for it is near the UNESCO headquarters, the Invalides air terminal, and on the right bank, the Champs-Elysées.

FROM UNESCO HOUSE TO PORTE DE VERSAILLES

At the heart of the triangle formed by Beaugrenelle, Montparnasse Tower and the Porte de Versailles, the 15th arrondissement, cut through by the rue Lecourbe and the rue de Vaugirard, is mostly a district where people stop on their way to the large business centres. For many years it has been a district of craftsmen and shopkeepers, and it has changed a lot over the past twenty years. The last urbanistic project to take place is the Javel embankments on the Front de Seine.

<u>RIVE DROITE - RIGHT BANK</u>

TROCADERO

Above the Seine river, the Trocadero widely opens onto a vast view of the Eiffel Tower, the Champ de Mars and the Ecole Militaire. From here, avenues radiate through the entire 16th arrondissement so that the Trocadero links Auteuil to the Etoile. There are also many museums nearby, and it is the starting point for architectural walks during which you'll discover Guimard's Art Nouveau creations, the art deco realizations of Le Corbusier, Sauvage, Mallet Stevens, Jeanneret and Perret.

PORTE MAILLOT

The Porte Maillot, and what has made it a business centre, the Palais des Congrès, is borded by the West ring road and the Bois de Boulogne, and is halfway between the Etoile and La Défense. It has the advantage of being in Paris, without suffering from the city's main problem : traffic jams.

ETOILE - CHAMPS-ELYSEES

This district is the link between La Défense and the Grand Louvre, it is a business centre as well as a commercial area and is famous for its night-life ; all along the avenue you'll see cafés, shopping malls, cinemas and night-clubs. At the Rond Point, this setting is replaced by quiet gardens, theatres, and the Grand and Petit Palais museums.

MADELEINE - OPERA

A business and shopping centre where banks, stores, travel agencies and duty-free shops stand next to one another, and a district where from the Opera to the Salle Favart, theatres and concert halls are countless. You can also discover, from the passage Choiseul to the rue Réaumur, the first glass and metal architectural creations : banks and stores, passages near the Grands Boulevards.

TUILERIES - LOUVRE

The Louvre Palace and the Tuileries Gardens are at the end of the long perspective which starts at the Etoile. This district is both very elegant and popular, a business and a cultural area, extremely animated in the daytime and in the evening. It is a very agreeable, lively and central district close to everything : the Palais Royal has gone back into fashion thanks to the architect Buren, and the Louvre museum with the pyramid designed by Peï.

CHATELET - LES HALLES

This area has completely changed since the central market ("halles" in French) was transferred to Rungis and the Forum was built. It is an enormous shopping mall which has attracted the "up-to-date" fashion designers and numerous cafés and restaurants. The Montorgueil market, several beautiful churches and the Fontaine des Innocents are still there to remind us of the past of this district. Southward, the Seine river and two theatres : Châtelet and Sarah Bernhardt.

MARAIS - BASTILLE

Between Beaubourg and the Bastille, the Marais displays a series of beautiful town houses and squares (among which the famous place des Vosges), museums and old houses to which the animated rues de Rivoli and Saint-Antoine give the rythm of life. Westward, there is Beaubourg which has attracted the creation of an artistic centre and where the majority of modern art galleries have taken up residence. At the other end, the Bastille, the new Opera and a recent area for modern art is set between the rues de Lappe and de la Roquette.

TRAIN STATIONS : SAINT-LAZARE, NORD, EST

One has to be a true Parisian to know this district, surrounded by the Grands Boulevards. However, public squares, small passageways and theatres are numerous in this district to which the 19th century gave its present shape. Near the Trinité church, a small area called "New Athens", was, for a while a meeting place for artists and writers. Here you'll discover an extremely original museum : the Gustave Moreau museum.

MONTMARTRE

Montmartre is not a district out of a light opera but a real village showing the spirit of authentic solidarity. Up here everything is charming, the names of the streets (allée des Brouillards, rue Sainte-Rustique), the inhabitants (artists and people who have lived here for generations), the transportation (funicular, minibus) and even its graveyard. All the routes are pretty, from the avenue Junot to the rue du Chevalier-de-la-Barre, from the Moulin de la Galette to the rue Saint-Vincent.

NATION - PERE LACHAISE

The boulevards Philippe-Auguste and Ménilmontant link the place de la Nation to the Père Lachaise running along small gardens and houses. The street names witness of a revolutionary past when this area was a village. Two famous cemetaries punctuate this district both popular and authentic : the little Picpus cemetary, where rests the French aristocracy guillotined on the place de la Nation (named place du Trône Renversé in 1793) and the Père Lachaise, immense and grand, where celebrities lie close from Chopin to Sarah Bernhardt, Colette or Simone Signoret.

OUTLYING DISTRICTS OF PARIS

FORET D'ERMENONVILLE

Between Senlis, one of the most beautiful French towns, and the abbey of Châalis, the serenity of a region where cultivations and forests are in balance. In Ermenonville, the memory of Rousseau haunts a romantic park with "factories" showing the imagination of 18th century aesthetes.

FORETS DE CHANTILLY ET DE COMPIEGNE

Well kept up, dotted with forest farms, the forest of Chantilly and Compiègne make you want to walk and in the fall, you shall see deers at the rutting season. Staghunt, riding, race season in a preserved region where Blanche de Castille once decided to build the abbey of Royaumont.

VALLEES DE LA BRIE

Through this wheat-growing land flows the Marne river, along which sigthseeing is becoming more and more popular, especially if you make a few stops to taste good cuisine. Further down, the more hidden valleys of Grand and Petit Morin show some very beautiful sights with the charm of old windmills.

FORET DE FONTAINEBLEAU

One of the biggest French forests where walking is an occasion to discover a large variety of trees and rocks. Pretty villages where painters moved (like Barbizon), with churches from the Middle Ages, the Loing and Seine rivers, Fontainebleau (its castle and the stairs leading to the Horseshoe) are so many wonderful sights.

VALLEES DU GATINAIS

This vast plateau is also a country of mixed woodland and pasture-land lying between the valleys of Lunain and Orvanne. Some charming *villages, rivers and ponds abounding with fish, churches and castles give character to this region.*

Hostellerie du Moulin de Flagy : 77940 Flagy ❀ 162

VALLEES DE LA BEAUCE

One of France's granary with Etampes as its chief-town, it used to be the royal city at the time of the Capetians. Southward, the Juine, the Louette and the Chalouette rivers create a green route among woods and hills. Something worth a detour is the domaine de Jeurre, its park shelters ruins of ancient buildings and picturesque "factories".

Hostellerie de Villemartin : Villemartin - 91150 Morigny ❀ 163

VALLEE DE CHEVREUSE

A regional park with something unreal to it, this region south of Versailles has managed to preserve the quality of its environment. From Dampierre to Chevreuse, from the abbey of Port-Royal-des-Champs to the abbey of Vaux de Cernay, castles, monasteries, small ancient towns among vales and woods witness the cultural past of the Ile-de-France.

Auberge du Gros Marronnier : 78720 Senlisse ❀ 164
Auberge du Pont Hardi : 78720 Senlisse ❀ 165
Abbaye des Vaux de Cernay : Cernay-la-Ville - 78720 Dampierre ❀ ..166

FORET DE RAMBOUILLET

Ancient trees, ponds, beautiful forest farms and villages are as many a worthwhile stop in this forest of Rambouillet. Two charming towns draw the limits to this region : Monfort-l'Amaury to the north, Rambouillet to the south, with a shoot in the immense park of the castle.

Château-hôtel du Tremblay-sur-Mauldre : 78490 Montfort-l'Amaury ❀ ..167

VALLEE DE LA SEINE

Northwest of Paris, the Seine river unwinds its peaceful meanders along a valley which looks like an orchard. Poissy, Orgeval, Meulun, Mantes-la-Jolie show the intense work which went on along the river in centuries past.

Le Moulin d'Orgeval : 78630 Orgeval ❀ 168

NORMANDIE

Vernon, the atmosphere is already that of the Norman countryside, in the gardens with ponds and the house of Monet in Giverny. Slightly up north, Les Andelys, with its back to the chalky cliffs on the border of the Seine river, witnesses with Château Gaillard, of the battles between Frenchmen and Englishmen to rule over this province.

Château de Brécourt : 27120 Douains ❀ 169
Hostellerie La Chaîne d'Or : 27700 Les Andelys ❀ 170
Hôtel de Normandie : 27700 Les Andelys ❀ 171

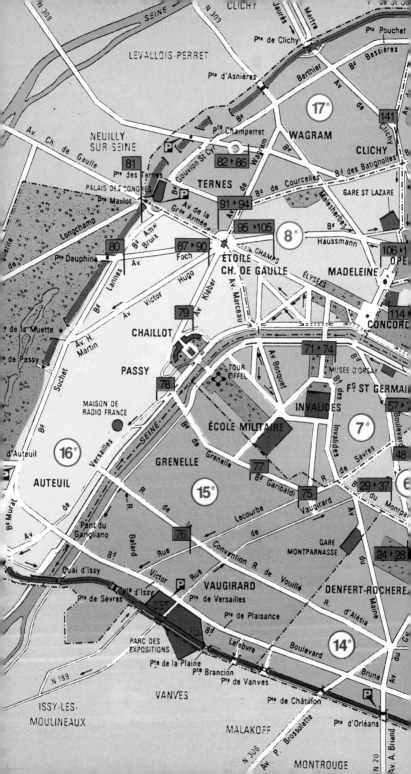

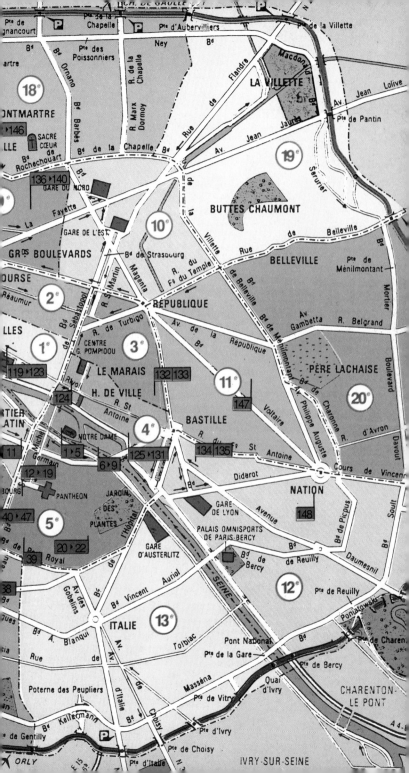

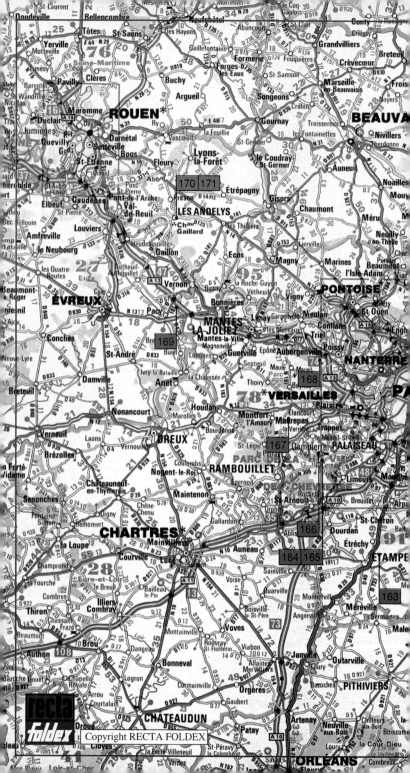

Hôtel de Notre-Dame ★★★

19 rue Maître-Albert - 75005 Paris
Tel. : (1) 43 26 79 00 - Telex : 205 060 - Fax : (1) 46 33 50 11
Manager : Mr Fouhety

♦ *34 sound-proofed rooms with shower or bath, direct dial line, cable TV, hair-drier and minibar* ♦ *Prices : double with shower : 510 F, with bath : 550 to 750 F - Extra bed : 200 F* ♦ *Breakfast with orange juice : 40 F* ♦ *Off-season : December, January, from 15 July to 15 August* ♦ *Facilities : reservations, laundry, dry-cleaning* ♦ *No dogs allowed* ♦ *Parking facilities : 1 rue Lagrange* ♦ *Transportation : Metro station Saint-Michel, RER Cluny-Saint-Michel - Buses 21, 24, 27, 38, 47, 85 and 96.*

On one side, the rue Maître-Albert offers a view on Notre-Dame, on the other, begins the montagne Sainte-Geneviève, topped by the Panthéon. Faithful to this location very "old Paris", the hotel has adopted a classical style livened up by a magnificent tapestry and several pretty pieces of furniture. Deep sofas, big bunches of flowers, partitions with openwork design, give comfort and character to the place.

Dark-blue *chiné* moquette, walls lined with pastel-coloured buckskin, beams, contemporary furniture of light oak veneer and charming shades for the fabrics of the curtains and bedspreads : these materials are simple but of quality and make the rooms very agreeable. Nice bathrooms separated from the room by a tiny Japanese-like partition.

Most welcoming, in a pretty and quiet street, this hotel is excellent.

Le Notre-Dame Hôtel ★★★

1, quai Saint-Michel - 75005 Paris
Tel. : (1) 43 54 20 43 - Telex : 206 650 - Fax : (1) 43 20 98 72
Manager : Mr Rols

♦ *23 rooms and 3 duplex apt., sound-proofed, with shower or bath, direct dial line, TV and minibar* ♦ *Bar* ♦ *Prices : single or double with shower or bath : 540 to 740 F ; duplex apt. : 1 000 F* ♦ *Breakfast with orange juice : 35 F* ♦ *Off-season : January and February* ♦ *Credit cards : American Express, Diners and Visa* ♦ *Facilities : reservations, laundry, dry-cleaning* ♦ *No dogs allowed* ♦ *Parking facilities : Parvis Notre-Dame* ♦ *Transportation : Metro station Saint-Michel, RER Cluny-Saint-Michel - Buses 21, 24, 27, 38, 47, 85 and 96.*

The intense traffic reigning at the crossroads between the Saint-Michel embankment and the rue Saint-Jacques where the hotel stands, seems dissuasive at first. But this would be a mistake : protected by double picture windows, this hotel benefits from complete quiet, with a postcard-like view of the Seine riverbanks and Notre-Dame Cathedral. You have to go up to the first floor to find the lobby and the lounge-bar. A plum-coloured moquette, salmon pink fabrics for tapestries and armchairs, a small lamp on each table, engravings of the old Paris and a fireplace are combined with a polite welcome. The rooms (they all look out onto the embankments and Notre-Dame Cathedral, except for those whose number ends with 5) are very well sound-proofed, papered in green, pink or blue, depending on the floor, and furnished in a half rustic, half Louis-Philippe style, pleasant and cosy. More like Parisian one-room flats than like hotel rooms the apartments are a success : mezzanine, large attic windows offering a plunging view on Notre-Dame. Take a look at the old-fashioned French plumbing in the bathrooms. At the heart of Paris, this hotel is extremely welcoming.

Hôtel Le Colbert ★★★

7 rue de l'Hôtel-Colbert - 75005 Paris
Tel. : (1) 43 25 85 65 - Telex : 260 690 - Fax : (1) 43 25 80 19
Manager : Mr Canteloup

♦ *40 rooms with shower or bath, direct dial line, TV, hair-drier, safe and minibar* ♦ *Bar, conference room* ♦ *Prices : single or double : 955 F ; triple : 1 450 F ; suite : 1 755 F* ♦ *Breakfast with orange juice : 49 F* ♦ *Off-season : January, February and August* ♦ *Credit cards : American Express, Eurocard, MasterCard and Visa* ♦ *Facilities : reservations, laundry, dry-cleaning* ♦ *No dogs allowed* ♦ *Parking facilities : 1 rue Lagrange* ♦ *Transportation : Metro stations Saint-Michel and Maubert-Mutualité, RER Cluny-Saint-Michel - Buses 21, 24, 27, 38, 47, 85 and 96.*

In a district once considered working class, but now residential, the Colbert is an elegant 17th century pastiche and in no way does it mar the area.

Very classic, this hotel chose comfort with cretonne prints in blue and pink pastel shades, Régence furniture and alcoves compose an impeccable setting lacking some imagination.

Choose the rooms whose number ends with 2, they look out onto the embankments' poplars and the apse of Notre-Dame Cathedral ; if this is not possible, stay in room #47 facing the wonderful cupola of the first theatre of anatomy, restored a few years ago. This room is well worth the top floor apartment with its view on Notre-Dame Cathedral. A large living room-bar, all blue, is the last touch to this very proper hotel (which has become very expensive !), where you'll only hear soft voices.

Hôtel Esmeralda ★★

4 rue Saint-Julien-le-Pauvre - 75005 Paris
Tel. : (1) 43 54 19 20 - Telex : 270 105
Manager : Mrs Bruel

♦ *19 rooms with washbasins, shower or bath, direct dial line* ♦ *No lift or breakfast room* ♦ *Prices : single : 280 to 380 F ; double : 280 to 420 F ; suite : 540 F - Extra bed : 60 F* ♦ *Breakfast : 35 F* ♦ *No off-season* ♦ *No credit cards accepted* ♦ *Facilities : reservations* ♦ *Dogs allowed* ♦ *Parking facilities : 1 rue Lagrange, Maubert and Notre-Dame* ♦ *Transportation : Metro station Saint-Michel, RER Cluny-Saint-Michel - Buses 21, 24, 27, 38, 47, 85 and 96.*

Mrs Bruel is a magician who has decided to inhabit the Hôtel Esmeralda. Out of a small and ugly hotel, she made one of Paris most delicious hotel. Artists know it, they come, came or will do so, to take a look at the view : the square Saint-Julien-le-Pauvre and Notre-Dame Cathedral, also because of the most poetic rooms.

Well polished floor tiles follow the more or less even plane of the landings ; different wallpapers, light-coloured wainscoting cover the walls of the corridors, bathrooms and bedrooms, these are not very modern but nicely furnished with personal taste and Flee market finds : clocks, mirrors, round tables, white wooden dressing tables, bergere armchairs, swan-necked beds, candlesticks...

If you can, take a room with bath, they all give on Notre-Dame Cathedral.

In her small sitting room filled with papers, books and interesting objects, Mrs Bruel draws, writes and watches over the house.

Hôtel Parc Saint-Séverin ★★★

22 rue de la Parcheminerie - 75005 Paris
Tel. : (1) 43 54 32 17 - Telex : 270 905 - Fax : (1) 43 54 70 71
Manager : Mr Lingrand

♦ *27 sound-proofed rooms with bath, direct dial line, TV and minibar* ♦ *Prices : single : 400 F ; double : 500 to 1 400 F* ♦ *Breakfast : 40 F* ♦ *Off-season : August* ♦ *Credit cards : American Express, Eurocard, MasterCard and Visa* ♦ *Facilities : reservations, laundry, dry-cleaning, snacks* ♦ *No dogs allowed* ♦ *Parking facilities : Parvis Notre-Dame and 1 rue Lagrange* ♦ *Transportation : Metro station Cluny, RER Cluny-Saint-Michel - Buses 21, 24, 27, 47, 63, 86, 87 and 96.*

Located in one of Paris oldest districts (the Cluny thermae are but two steps away) and most animated (the boulevard Saint-Michel is nearby) the building faces the flamboyant church of Saint-Séverin. Renovated with rigour, under the authority of Mr Lingrand, also the owner of the Hôtel des Saint-Pères, this establishment is decorated in 1930s style, which has been very fashionable over the past few years. Grey from cellar to attic, this hotel makes use of just enough colours or beautiful objects to animate the decoration as a whole. All the rooms are of a good size and cosy with refined white, pink or grey bathrooms. Ask for the corner rooms, they have a double exposure, with a view on the church and the boulevard Saint-Germain, those on the sixth floor with a balcony or the large ones on the fifth floor, there is also a room on the seventh floor with a terrace : all look out onto the roofs of Paris and in the distance, you'll see Notre-Dame Cathedral or the Panthéon. This hotel is well managed in a more and more residential district.

Hôtel du Jeu de Paume ★★★★

54 rue Saint-Louis-en-l'Ile - 75004 Paris
Tel. : (1) 43 26 14 18 - Telex : 205 160 - Fax : (1) 43 26 14 18
Manager : Mrs Prache

♦ *32 rooms with bath, direct dial line, TV, hair-drier and minibar*
♦ *Patio, conference room, bar, relaxation room with sauna*
♦ *Prices : double : 700 to 940 F ; triple : 990 F - Extra bed : 150 F*
♦ *Breakfast : 65 F* ♦ *Off-season : winter (exclusive of professional shows)* ♦ *Credit cards : American Express, Diners, JCB and Visa* ♦ *Facilities : reservations, laundry, dry-cleaning, snacks, secretarial work* ♦ *Dogs allowed* ♦ *Parking facilities : 2 rue Geoffroy-l'Asnier and Parvis Notre-Dame* ♦ *Transportation : Metro station Pont-Marie - Buses 24, 63, 67, 86 and 87.*

An extraordinarily successful renovation transformed this former "jeu de paume" into a high quality hotel. Ceilings, partition walls, everything was torn down so as to leave a superb space with stone walls supporting a splendid structure. You have to take the lift, with windows on three sides, in order to discover one by one the hanging galleries used as landings to the rooms, the reading room on the mezzanine floor, the large, ancient ceramic tiles of the ground floor and the lounge-bar where on either side of the fireplace are two leather sofas. The ochre walls, the honey-coloured stones, and the Provençal furniture in the breakfast corner confer a Mediterranean touch that is enhanced by the patio onto which most of the rooms open. The rooms are tastefully decorated : subtle-grey walls, soft-coloured prints, beautiful beams, and modern furniture in light wood. Some of the rooms were designed to form a duplex apartment, and their marble bathrooms are often lit by a window. The welcome in this hotel is beyond reproach and breakfast, like in a dream : fresh fruits or juices, toast, honey and homemade jams...

Hôtel des Deux Iles ★★★

59 rue Saint-Louis-en-l'Ile - 75004 Paris
Tel. : (1) 43 26 13 35 - Fax : (1) 43 29 60 25
Manager : Mrs Buffat

♦ *17 sound-proofed rooms with shower or bath, direct dial line,
TV, hair-drier* ♦ *Bar* ♦ *Prices : single : 550 F ; double : 650 F*
♦ *Breakfast : 37 F* ♦ *No credit cards accepted* ♦ *Facilities :
reservations, laundry, dry-cleaning, snacks* ♦ *No dogs allowed*
♦ *Parking facilities : 2 rue Geoffroy-l'Asnier and Parvis Notre-
Dame* ♦ *Transportation : Metro station Pont-Marie - Buses 24,
63, 67, 86 and 87.*

At the heart of the Ile Saint-Louis, this engaging hotel is decorated
in an Indian Colonial style. Against a background of natural-
coloured fabric for the walls, the beams blend in harmoniously as do
the well waxed floor tiles, the luminous yellow curtains, the sofas
covered in big flowered chintz, and the green and yellow ceramic
tiles of the fountain which occupies the flowered light well. A few
exotic touches recall the tropics : over the patio window is drawn a
blind with fine slats, a bird cage is in a corner, two green straw-
bottomed chairs, some plants. This decoration is such a success that
you immediately feel as if you had plunged into a different world.
You will also feel the fragrance of this atmosphere in the rooms
(quite small) with bamboo and cane furniture painted blue or yellow
depending on the dominant colour of the room, and with Provençal
prints for the curtains and bedspreads ; this atmosphere pervades
even the bathrooms tiled in blue ceramic. In the vaulted basement,
where breakfast is served, there is a pretty fireplace. In the afternoon
this becomes a bar where drinks are served until late at night. A nice
hotel with its very own atmosphere.

Hôtel de Lutèce ★★★

65 rue Saint-Louis-en-l'Ile - 75004 Paris
Tel. : (1) 43 26 23 52 - Fax : (1) 43 29 60 25
Manager : Mr Buffat

♦ *23 rooms with bath, direct dial line and* TV ♦ *Prices : single :
550 F ; double : 660 F ; triple : 900 F* ♦ *Breakfast : 38 F* ♦ *Off-
season : winter (exclusive of professional shows)* ♦ *No credit
cards accepted* ♦ *Facilities : reservations, laundry, dry-cleaning
♦ No dogs allowed* ♦ *Parking facilities : 2 rue Geoffroy-l'Asnier
and Parvis Notre-Dame* ♦ *Transportation : Metro stations Pont-
Marie and Hôtel-de-Ville - Buses 24, 63, 67, 86 and 87.*

Nowhere else will you find such a pretty lobby as the one in this old
house turned into a hotel : a high stone fireplace in a corner,
beautiful furniture, old floor tiles well waxed and a magnificent
bunch of flowers create a general impression of quality. On each
landing there is a fine object : an antique table, a pretty faience in a
cabinet or a mirror elegantly framed. The rooms are less
exceptional, apart from two sixth floor rooms with sloping ceilings,
still the others, though small, are nice, with beams, pebble-dashed
walls and charming print curtains. A refined hotel in the best known
"village" of Paris.

Hôtel Saint-Louis ★★

75 rue Saint-Louis-en-l'Ile - 75004 Paris
Tel. : (1) 46 34 04 80 - Fax : (1) 46 34 02 13
Manager : Mrs Record

♦ *21 sound-proofed rooms with shower or bath, direct dial line, hair-drier and safe* ♦ *Prices : double with double bed : 510 F, with twin beds : 610 F - Extra bed : 180 F* ♦ *Breakfast : 39 F* ♦ *No credit cards accepted* ♦ *Facilities : reservations, laundry* ♦ *Small dogs allowed* ♦ *Parking facilities : 2 rue Geoffroy-l'Asnier, Parvis Notre-Dame and Hôtel-de-Ville* ♦ *Transportation : Metro station Pont-Marie, RER Cluny-Saint-Michel - Buses 24, 63, 67, 86 and 87.*

A special hotel in this extremely civilized village of the Ile Saint-Louis.

In the lobby the decoration is definitely Medieval, the russet of the floor tiles, beams and columns and the beige of the stone walls harmonized with the deep-blue colour of the seats, curtains and lampshades, the whole being set to advantage by soft lights and big bouquets. The same decor is to be found in the basement where breakfast is served.

Clean, amazingly silent with walls lined in soft pink, the rooms are kept up by Mrs Record with love. Here the furniture is nice and has style. No television for the management is firmly opposed to it !

But if you show but a little interest, you can chat at the reception desk and find out everything about this neighbourhood (well worth it !). Welcoming and simple, this hotel is also comfortable and attractive.

Hôtel Relais Christine ★★★★

3 rue Christine - 75006 Paris
Tel. : (1) 43 26 71 80 - Telex : 202 606 - Fax : (1) 43 26 89 38
Manager : Mr Regnault

♦ *34 rooms and 17 duplex apt., sound-proofed and air-conditioned, with bath, direct dial line, TV, hair-drier and minibar* ♦ *Garden, conference room, garage (25 spaces)* ♦ *Prices : single or double : 1 200 F ; triple : 1 800 F ; duplex apt. : 1 600 to 2 200 F* ♦ *Breakfast with orange or grapefruit juices : 80 F* ♦ *Off-season : August* ♦ *Credit cards : American Express, Diners and Visa* ♦ *Facilities : reservations, laundry, dry-cleaning, snacks* ♦ *Dogs allowed* ♦ *Parking facilities : private garage* ♦ *Transportation : Metro stations Odéon or Saint-Michel, RER Cluny-Saint-Michel - Buses 24, 27, 58, 63, 70, 86, 87 and 96.*

A nice gate opening on a flowered courtyard and a garden surrounded by walls enclose this establishment. The building itself used to be an Augustin monastery. This hotel is appealing on sight because of its welcoming atmosphere, quite uncommon for a place of this category.

The decoration is warm and amusing, the panelled lounge looks very much like a gallery of family portraits. These were bought from a specialist at the beginning of the century. In the rooms the walls are covered with sienna or brick-coloured fabrics brightened by a white stitch, their atmosphere is restful. The bathrooms of natural marble are of a good size. Here, comfort never yields to gratuitous aestheticism. If you can, take a room giving on the garden (which is closed, unfortunately) or a suite on the top floor ; but everything is agreeable in this high quality hotel ; like its twin brother the Pavillon de la Reine, it has the elegance of simplicity.

Left Bank Hôtel ★★★

9 rue de l'Ancienne-Comédie - 75006 Paris
Tel. : (1) 43 54 01 70 - Telex : 200 502 - Fax : (1) 43 26 17 14
Manager : Mr Teil

♦ *30 rooms and 1 suite, sound-proofed and air-conditioned, with bath, direct dial line, TV by satellite, hair-drier, safe and minibar* ♦ *Prices : single or double : 850 to 1 050 F ; suite : 1 200 F - Extra bed : 150 F* ♦ *Breakfast included* ♦ *Off-season : 15 November to 15 February (exclusive of professional shows)* ♦ *Credit cards : American Express, Diners and Visa* ♦ *Facilities : reservations, laundry, dry-cleaning* ♦ *Dogs allowed* ♦ *Parking facilities : opposite 21 rue de l'Ecole-de-Médecine and 27 rue Mazarine* ♦ *Transportation : Metro station Odéon, RER Cluny-Saint-Michel - Buses 58, 63, 70, 86, 87 and 96.*

We had kept an eye on this hotel which opened a year ago and was being renovated, but its location in a very busy street had discouraged us to visit it once the work was over.

We were wrong : if you like this day-and-night lively district, and if you choose, in the summer, the rooms on the courtyard side or giving on the passage du Commerce-Saint-André, you will appreciate without mental reservation the qualities of this perfectly sound-proofed and ultra-comfortable house, with small terraces opening onto flowered backyards (unfortunately inaccessible).

Faithful to their taste for tapestry, exposed beams, oak panelling, velvet, paisley patterns, copies of old paintings and Louis XIII furniture, Mr and Mrs Teil succeeded, here also, a classic and warm decoration where you feel at ease. Same taste for details in the bathrooms covered with marble, and pretty mirrors in wooden frames. Nice little things such as miniature sewing kits, generous breakfasts : a nice place, where the prices could be more reasonnable.

Select Hôtel ★★★

1 place de la Sorbonne - 75005 Paris
Tel. : (1) 46 34 14 80 - Telex : 201 207 - Fax : (1) 46 34 51 79
Manager : Mr Chabrerie

♦ *69 rooms with shower or bath, direct dial line and* TV ♦ *Bar with terrace on the square in summer* ♦ *Prices : single : 460 to 580 F ; double : 540 to 660 F ; triple : 790 F* ♦ *Breakfast included* ♦ *Off-season : July and August* ♦ *Credit cards : American Express, Diners and Visa* ♦ *Facilities : reservations, laundry, dry-cleaning* ♦ *Dogs allowed* ♦ *Parking facilities : 20 rue Soufflot* ♦ *Transportation : Metro stations Saint-Michel or Odéon, RER Luxembourg or Cluny-Saint-Michel - Buses 21, 27, 38, 63, 82, 84, 86 and 87.*

From the outside it looks like a spruce little establishment, but once through the door, the high glass pyramid set over the interior garden proves that nothing is old-fashioned here. Light comes from above the flowers and the fountain. In the basement, the breakfast room (where fresh fruits, juices and cereals are served together with your continental breakfast, all this free of charge). On a mezzanine, the reception desk where the staff is comely.

Classic style takes over in the bedrooms, all are of a good size even the smaller ones : beams, flowered, soft-coloured Japanese wallpapers or exposed stones, large wardrobes, brown wooden modern furnishing, well arranged bathrooms, now with beige or grey marble, now with small tiles, blue or green. On the sixth floor, from the rooms on the street side you can see the attic windows and chimneys of the Sorbonne and you can hear its chapel's discreet chimes. The back rooms have a view on the red ochre of newly painted walls, humourously decorated with ivy lianas in... plastic. The rooms overlooking the square are very bright and protected from the commotion of the boulevard Saint-Michel by plane trees.

Le Jardin de Cluny ★★★

9 rue du Sommerard - 75005 Paris
Tel. : (1) 43 54 22 66 - Telex : 206 975 - Fax : (1) 40 51 03 36
Manager : Mr Condy

♦ 40 rooms with shower or bath, direct dial line, TV by satellite , hair-drier and minibar ♦ Prices : single with shower : 480 F, with bath : 520 F ; double with shower : 535 F, with bath : 650 F ; suite : 860 F - Extra bed : 135 F ♦ Breakfast with orange juice and cheese : included ♦ Off-season : winter (exclusive of professional shows) ♦ Credit cards : American Express, Diners and Visa ♦ Facilities : reservations, laundry, dry-cleaning ♦ No dogs allowed ♦ Parking facilities : 1 rue Lagrange ♦ Transportation : Metro station Maubert-Mutualité, RER Cluny-Saint-Michel - Buses 21, 24, 27, 47, 63, 85, 86 and 87.

A white façade in a quiet street within a stone's throw from the Cluny museum and the Sorbonne, this hotel is a bit isolated from the noisy corner where the boulevards Saint-Michel and Saint-Germain meet. In the lobby the materials are smooth and shining and in summertime, a wide window opens on a flowered light well. Two tall neo-Babylonian bowmen in blue enamelled brick guard the stairway leading to the basement ; there, you'll find the breakfast room and the lounge-bar (where blue predominates), which can easily be turned into a conference room.
In the bedrooms the colours are brick, rose, blue or green enhanced by bright print curtains and bedspreads. Lacquered bamboo bedheads and furniture, small paintings of Indian inspiration hang on the walls. The bathrooms are newly redone. The sixth floor with sloping ceilings is particularly nice. On the whole this is a pretty, well done and restful hotel.

Hôtel Plaisant ★★

50 rue des Bernardins - 75005 Paris
Tel. : (1) 43 54 74 57
Manager : Mr Fardeau

♦ *24 rooms, sound-proofed on the street side, with washbasins or bath ; phone : through the swithchboard* ♦ *Prices : single or double with washbasins : 165 to 190 F, with shower : 320 F, with bath : 380 F* ♦ *Breakfast : 25 F* ♦ *Off-season : January and the last 2 weeks of August* ♦ *No credit cards accepted* ♦ *Facilities : reservations* ♦ *Dogs allowed* ♦ *Parking facilities : 1 rue Lagrange* ♦ *Transportation : Metro stations Cardinal-Lemoine or Maubert-Mutualité, RER Cluny-Saint-Michel - Buses 47, 63, 86 and 87.*

Extraordinarily provincial, this hotel is at the opposite of the commotion of the boulevard Saint-Michel and lives quietly in the shade of the public square's trees, to the rythm of this district.

This does not mean it lacks character in any way : here, everything is unexpected, starting with the façade, built at the end of the 19th century, quite heavy, hidden in the summer by plants hanging from the balconies, to the Egyptian link downstairs.

Four neo-classic channeled columns and an enormous plant fills the small entrance. In the rooms, ornamental mouldings on the ceilings, mirrors with rococo frames, Alsacian stoves in faience or small fireplaces carefully looked after create an atmosphere protected from a standard renovation. The old-fashioned bathrooms are no less comfortable and very clean. The faithful customers have organized ch good verbal advertising that the hotel is full all year round. It is elcoming and quiet hotel, old-fashioned in a pretty way.

Hôtel des Grandes Ecoles ★★

75 rue du Cardinal-Lemoine - 75005 Paris
Tel. : (1) 43 26 79 23
Manager : Mrs Le Floch

◆ *48 rooms with washbasins, shower or bath, direct dial line* ◆ *Garden* ◆ *Prices : single or double : 280 to 500 F - Extra bed : 100 F* ◆ *Breakfast : 35 F* ◆ *Credit card : Visa* ◆ *Facilities : reservations* ◆ *Small dogs allowed* ◆ *Parking facilities : 20 rue Soufflot and place du Panthéon (no parking meters)* ◆ *Transportation : Metro stations Cardinal-Lemoine or Monge, RER Luxembourg - Buses 47, 84 and 89.*

People who have lived between the Contrescarpe district and the Panthéon still speak with words of breathless admiration about those three little houses which, at the end of a blind alley, give on an abundant and fragrant garden. A lot of work was done lately, one of the houses was pulled down, another was enlarged, cutting through lilacs, bushes, plane trees and lindens. However, this hotel is still among the extraordinary places of Paris. Its appearance is now less pastoral (the vegetation will grow again !) but it is more comfortable and well heated. It stays out of time thanks to the management who hasn't changed. You have to walk through the garden, up the steps of the pink house, toward the lobby and the breakfast room with its wooden tables and cane chairs. The rooms are white, green, pink or blue, colours pervading the bathroom tiles. By chance, some of them kept their original cotton print decoration, they are the prettiest : furnished in rustic or Louis-Philippe style with lace bedspreads. Unharmed, the last house still looks like a cottage, sheltered behind white barriers. The bathrooms are small but impeccable. Here also, several rooms kept the original cretonne print wallcovering, the others were renovated.

Hôtel des Grands Hommes ★★★

17 place du Panthéon - 75005 Paris
Tel. : (1) 46 34 19 60 - Telex : 200 185 - Fax : (1) 43 26 67 32
Manager : Miss Brethous

♦ *32 rooms with bath, direct dial line, cable TV, hair-drier and minibar* ♦ *Prices : single : from 580 F ; double : 700 F - Extra bed : 100 F* ♦ *Breakfast with orange juice : 30 F* ♦ *Off-season : winter (exclusive of professional shows)* ♦ *Credit cards : American Express, Diners, Eurocard, MasterCard and Visa* ♦ *Facilities : reservations, laundry, dry-cleaning* ♦ *Dogs allowed* ♦ *Parking facilities : 20 rue Soufflot and place du Panthéon (no parking meters)* ♦ *Transportation : Metro station Cardinal-Lemoine, RER Luxembourg - Buses 21, 27, 38, 82, 84, 85 and 89.*

The new decoration, neo-classic and 1930s style combined, was conceived for the smooth and pink lobby of this exquisite hotel near the Luxembourg Gardens.

The rooms are decorated in soft pastel colours, furnished with sometimes antique brass beds and English pieces of light tinted wood. The bathrooms, tiled in ceramic showing little brown patterns are a great success. On the top floor, the two rooms with sloping ceilings overlooking the square are just delightful : the ceilings are high notwithstanding the slope of the roof, their balconies are sufficiently large so that you can sit and eat breakfast in the summer, looking at one of Paris most beautiful views : the Panthéon and over the roofs the entire city up to the Sacré-Cœur which appears in the distance.

Hôtel du Panthéon ★★★

19 place du Panthéon - 75005 Paris
Tel. : (1) 43 54 32 95 - Telex : 206 435 - Fax : (1) 43 26 64 65
Manager : Miss Brethous

♦ *34 rooms, sound-proofed on the street side, with bath, direct dial line, cable TV, hair-drier and minibar* ♦ *Prices : single : from 580 F ; double : 700 F - Extra bed : 100 F* ♦ *Breakfast with orange juice : 30 F* ♦ *Off-season : winter (exclusive of professional shows) and August* ♦ *Credit cards : American Express, Diners, Eurocard, MasterCard and Visa* ♦ *Facilities : reservations, laundry, dry-cleaning* ♦ *Dogs allowed* ♦ *Parking facilities : place du Panthéon (no parking meters) and 20 rue Soufflot* ♦ *Transportation : Metro station Cardinal-Lemoine, RER Luxembourg - Buses 21, 27, 38, 82, 84, 85 and 89.*

Both the Hôtel du Panthéon and the Hôtel des Grands Hommes are held by the same family. It is therefore natural to find here the same spirit in the decoration with, of course, several differences. The pastel colours where blue predominates are the same, but in the hallway the decoration is more theatrical : two immaculate columns and a gate with small volutes in wrought iron separate, without closing it, the sitting room from the vestibule.

Louis XVI furnishing, alcoves, blue, beige or pink fabrics are used for the often small rooms. Those bearing numbers in 1 are bigger but they all are quiet and elegantly furnished.

The bathrooms match but in a brighter tonality the colours of the rooms, they are sometimes brightened by a large window. This is a good, classic and welcoming hotel.

Hôtel des Trois Collèges ★★

16 rue Cujas - 75005 Paris
Tel. : (1) 43 54 67 30 - Telex : 206 034 - Fax : (1) 46 34 02 99
Manager : Mrs Wyplosz

♦ *44 sound-proofed rooms with shower or bath, direct dial line, TV and hair-drier* ♦ *Prices : single : 290 F ; double with shower : 360 F, with bath : 410 F ; triple with bath : 650 F* ♦ *Breakfast with orange juice : 35 F* ♦ *Off-season : December and January* ♦ *Credit cards : American Express, Diners, En Route and Visa* ♦ *Facilities : reservations, laundry, dry-cleaning* ♦ *No dogs allowed* ♦ *Parking facilities : 20 rue Soufflot* ♦ *Transportation : Metro station Saint-Michel, RER Luxembourg and Cluny-Saint-Michel - Buses 21, 27, 38, 63, 82, 84, 86 and 87.*

In the shade of the Sorbonne and the Panthéon, the Hôtel des Trois Collèges attracts the eye with its newly painted façade and bright entrance : completely white walls, straight lines and light wood covering. But later a surprise awaits you : in the diffuse whiteness of the nearby dining room, where an enormous fern grows under a glass roof, you discover the stones of the coping of an old well, narrow and so very deep...

The lounge is sober and pretty : modern armchairs of light wood, white curtains, a bouquet in a tall 1900 vase. Same atmosphere in the rooms where the colours play a game of beige and white (even the tiles in the well equipped bathrooms), around light wooden furniture and a rust-coloured moquette. From the sixth floor with sloping ceilings where the largest rooms are, you'll see the Panthéon the Sorbonne. Remember also : pretty corner rooms (numbers ﹍g in 4), orange juice and homemade jams for breakfast ; here is ﹍ect 2-star, even the bill is !

Hôtel Saint-Paul ★★★

43 rue Monsieur-le-Prince - 75006 Paris
Tel. : (1) 43 26 98 64 - Telex : 203 257 - Fax : (1) 46 34 58 60
Manager : Mr Hawkins

♦ *31 rooms with shower or bath, direct dial line, TV, hair-drier and minibar* ♦ *Prices : single : 415 F ; double : 500 to 650 F* ♦ *Breakfast with orange juice : 35 F* ♦ *Off-season : first 2 weeks of February and December* ♦ *Credit cards : American Express, Diners and Visa* ♦ *Facilities : réservations and repassage* ♦ *No dogs allowed* ♦ *Parking facilities : 20 rue Soufflot and rue de l'Ecole-de-Médecine* ♦ *Transportation : Metro station Odéon, RER Luxembourg or Cluny-Saint-Michel - Buses 21, 27, 38, 63, 82, 84, 86 and 87.*

Right in the centre of the Latin Quarter, the rue Monsieur-le-Prince follows what used to be the city walls built by Philippe-Auguste ; its large stones were often used as a base for houses. At #43, a typically British cocktail awaits the coming guest : sense of humour, warmth and charm, served by Mr Hawkins, a Parisian Englishman who has been renovating with love this old house for the past ten years. Exposed beams and stones, furniture of warm tones in the lobby, lit by a copper centre light and a small light well. In the rooms (sizes varie), beams, 17th century comfortable furniture, plain fabrics or chintz for the walls and curtains ; always large closets and a desk ; here and there a mirror, a small painting or a canopy. Bathrooms are of white, red or pink marble. On the courtyard side, from the third floor up, the rooms overlook the Lycée Saint-Louis and take advantage of the plane trees growing on the playground. On each floor, pots of flowers and even young tomato plants grow bravely on the windowsills...

Hôtel du Jardin des Plantes ★★

5 rue Linné - 75005 Paris
Tel. : (1) 47 07 06 20 - Telex : 203 684 - Fax : (1) 47 07 62 74
Manager : Mrs Bompard

♦ *33 rooms with shower or bath, direct dial line, TV, hair-drier and minibar* ♦ *Flowered terrace , bar, tearoom, exhibition and concert room, sauna* ♦ *Prices : single : 320 to 520 F ; double : 360 to 560 F - Extra bed : 100 F* ♦ *Breakfast with orange juice : 35 F* ♦ *Off-season : January, February and August* ♦ *Credit cards : American Express, Diners, En Route, Eurocard, MasterCard and Visa* ♦ *Facilities : reservations, laundry, dry-cleaning, snacks* ♦ *Dogs allowed* ♦ *Parking facilities : 4 rue du Marché-des-Patriaches and 15 rue Censier* ♦ *Transportation : Metro station Jussieu, RER Gare d'Austerlitz - Buses 67 and 89.*

This five-storey narrow building looks like a naïve painting with its red and white striped blinds at the back of the Jardin des Plantes. Already in the entrance, it is obvious that this pretty and simple hotel was conceived for its guests' well-being. The rooms are a success (except on the dark ground floor). They are decorated in a pastoral style and according to each floor the motif changes : wistaria, bindweed, geranium, iris or mimosa. This decoration is completed by an extra piece of furniture, judicious lighting, a useful accessory. On the street side, there is a pleasant view on the Jardin des Plantes, but the other side, overlooking the courtyard, has its secret : a hanging terrace where you can breakfast in the sun during the summer and on which opens one of the fifth floor rooms. In the basement, a sauna, an ironing room and a vaulted room used as a lounge or a concert hall. On the ground floor, a bar-restaurant serves a large variety of teas and delicious snacks. You will quickly feel at home here.

Hôtel Résidence Saint-Christophe ★★★

17 rue Lacépède - 75005 Paris
Tel. : (1) 43 31 81 54 - Telex : 204 304 - Fax : (1) 43 31 12 54
Manager : Mrs Prétet

♦ *31 rooms with shower or bath, direct dial line,* TV, *hair-drier and minibar* ♦ *Prices : single : 550 F ; double : 600 F* ♦ *Breakfast with orange juice, cheese and cereals : 40 F* ♦ *Off-season : winter (exclusive of professional shows) and July-August* ♦ *Credit cards : Air+, American Express, Diners, JCB and Visa* ♦ *Facilities : reservations, laundry, dry-cleaning* ♦ *Dogs allowed* ♦ *Parking facilities : 4 rue du Marché-des-Patriarches and 15 rue Censier* ♦ *Transportation : Metro stations Monge or Jussieu, RER Gare d'Austerlitz - Buses 47, 67 and 89.*

The rue Lacépède leads directly to the Jardin des Plantes set between the Arènes de Lutèce and the mosque : quite a nice location for this hotel, renovated in 1987…

It is quite nice upon arrival, a beautiful Louis XV desk rural style, marble flooring and a peach colour which is the leitmotiv of this hotel's decoration. The lounge with armchairs and lights arranged in a 1930s fashion has a most restful atmosphere. Light-pink walls, quilted bedspreads and curtains of the same shade with grey, white and pink prints make a decor half-Régence, half-rustic for the rooms. Brass wall lamps and lamps ; good closets ; some alcoves (room numbers ending with 4). Modern bathrooms of beige marble. When the weather is nice, choose the rooms overlooking the rue de La Clef which is less busy ; otherwise if you are with your family take the rooms whose numbers end with 5 and 6, they communicate. The faithful clientele appreciates the importance accorded to the reception. A good hotel in a wonderful area.

Résidence Les Gobelins ★★

9 rue des Gobelins - 75013 Paris
Tel. : (1) 47 07 26 90 - Telex : 206 566 - Fax : (1) 43 31 44 05
Managers : Mr and Mrs Poirier

♦ *32 rooms with shower or bath, direct dial line and TV (Canal+)*
♦ *Patio* ♦ *Prices : single : 300 F ; double : 350 to 400 F - Extra bed : 130 F* ♦ *Breakfast with orange juice : 30 F* ♦ *Off-season : February and August* ♦ *Credit cards : American Express, Diners, Eurocard, MasterCard and Visa* ♦ *Facilities : reservations* ♦ *Dogs allowed* ♦ *Parking facilities : 60 boulevard Saint-Marcel and 1 rue Lagrange* ♦ *Transportation : Metro station Gobelins, RER Port-Royal - Buses 27, 47, 83 and 91.*

This old district of dyers where lived the Gobelin family, who gave their name to the King's manufacture (situated a few streets away from the hotel), still is a "village" with character. The hotel stands in a quiet street near the rue Mouffetard and the Jardin des Plantes.

The agreeable lobby-lounge is furnished with simple light wood sofas. Next to it, there is a breakfast room with flowered tablecloths and cane chairs, it opens on a garden filled with honeysuckles. Here, in the summer, people sit on wooden chairs with white cushions, under sunshades...

Everything in the rooms is blue, green or orange, even the furniture. They are of a reasonable size, even the smaller ones, and as it is often the case in Paris the sixth floor rooms have sloping ceilings. Almost all the back rooms on the top floors offer an unexpected sight : an abandonned garden, where several rabbits seem to live ! ̄ hotel is really loved by its staff, and they know how to share eling.

Hôtel du Parc Montsouris ★★

4 rue du Parc-Montsouris - 75014 Paris
Tel. : (1) 45 89 09 72 - Telex : 206 670 - Fax : (1) 45 80 92 72
Managers : Messr Trotignon and Grand

♦ *35 rooms with shower or bath, direct dial line, TV and minibar*
♦ *Conference room* ♦ *Prices : single or double with shower :*
300 F, with bath : 330 to 410 F ; suite : 470 F - Extra bed : 60 F
♦ *Breakfast with orange juice : 25 F (35 F in the room)* ♦ *Off-season : 15 December to March and August* ♦ *Credit cards :*
American Express, Diners and Visa ♦ *Facilities : reservations,*
laundry, snacks ♦ *Small dogs allowed* ♦ *Parking facilities :*
private alley ♦ *Transportation : Metro station Porte d'Orléans,*
RER Cité Universitaire - Orly Airport bus : Porte d'Orléans -
Buses PC, 27 and 47.

This little house was built in the 1920s, it has a white façade with stone balconies. It stands near the Parc Montsouris in one of Paris prettiest "hamlets"... Delightfully calm, surrounded by villas and gardens, but only five minutes away from the Porte de Versailles, this hotel benefits from an exceptional location. Inside unfortunately, nothing is left from what used to give charm to this house. The renovation work is on its way and has privileged lead-white wood and pastel shades, very fashionable nowadays in the hotel business.

The rooms are rigourously clean and comfortable, the bathrooms are well equipped. However, there are several good ideas : rooms with a sitting room corner, a new conference room and, last but not least, the professional welcome. A hotel which does its best to become a precious address.

Hôtel L'Aiglon ★★★

232 boulevard Raspail - 75014 Paris
Tel. : (1) 43 20 82 42 - Telex : 206 038 - Fax : (1) 43 20 98 72
Manager : Mr Rols

♦ *38 rooms and 9 suites, sound-proofed, with shower or bath, direct dial line, TV and minibar* ♦ *Prices : single : 400 F ; double : 460 to 600 F ; suite : 650 to 800 F - Extra bed : 100 F* ♦ *Breakfast : 32 F* ♦ *Off-season : winter (exclusive of professional shows)* ♦ *Credit cards : Air+, American Express, Diners, En Route, JCB and Visa* ♦ *Facilities : reservations, laundry, dry-cleaning, snacks* ♦ *Dogs allowed* ♦ *Parking facilities : 8 locked spaces in the hotel and 116 boulevard du Montparnasse* ♦ *Transportation : Metro station Raspail, RER and Orly Airport bus : Denfert-Rochereau - Bus 68, 83 and 91.*

1928 : Montparnasse lives in an artistic turmoil. A hotel is being built at the crossroads between the boulevards Raspail and Edgar-Quinet. Among the regulars you could see Luis Buñuel who loved the area. Easy to understand. The rooms are bathed with sunshine (we like best those overlooking the trees of the cemetery and the apartments with their small kitchen and price), their size is unusual and the clientele is very keen on its 1950s furniture. However, Mr Rols is transforming the house little by little : the lobby, bar, sitting room and dining room are all panelled in mahogany. On the last floors, furniture of cherry or spotted maple wood show on the clear hangings, curtains and bedspreads of woven cotton. Step by step this decoration will take up the entire hotel. However, we prefer the floors which kept their furniture of "modern post-war" style, impeccable and so funny with their steel base, Formica covering, paper lampshades… and the great leopard moquette!

Hôtel Istria ★★

29 rue Campagne-Première - 75014 Paris
Tel. : (1) 43 20 91 82 - Telex : 203 618 - Fax : (1) 43 22 48 45
Managers : Mr and Mrs Leroux

♦ *26 rooms, sound-proofed on the street side, with shower or bath, direct dial line, TV and safe* ♦ *Prices : single : 400 F ; double : 450 to 490 F - Extra bed : 100 F* ♦ *Breakfast with orange juice : 35 F* ♦ *Off-season : winter (exclusive of professional shows) and August* ♦ *Credit cards : American Express, Eurocard, MasterCard and Visa* ♦ *Facilities : reservations, laundry* ♦ *Dogs allowed* ♦ *Parking facilities : 116 boulevard du Montparnasse and boulevard Edgar-Quinet* ♦ *Transportation : Metro station Raspail, RER Denfert-Rochereau or Port-Royal - Orly Airport bus : Denfert-Rochereau - Bus 68, 83 and 91.*

In the authentic Montparnasse district, a pretty street and this hotel which used to be a small district establishment, it has just been renovated for the happiness of the neighbouring inhabitants who book rooms here for their friends from out of town. When cheap monthly tariffs still existed, Mayakovski, Rilke, Duchamp, Man Ray and Miller lived here. The conditions have changed but the bill is still reasonnable and the welcome, friendly. The hotel's original structures were not turned upside down, it is still intimate and unpretentious, and has become impeccable and comfortable. The lobby and the lounge were decorated in a comfortable and pleasant way. The rooms arn't large, but practical. The bathrooms are well equipped. The patchwork bedspreads remind you of the tablecloths in the breakfast room under a white stone vault. The pavilion in the backyard was also restored, the galleries running around it are now under a funny little glass roof ; here the rooms benefit from even more quiet...

Hôtel Raspail ★★★

203 boulevard Raspail - 75014 Paris
Tel. : (1) 43 20 62 86 - Fax : (1) 43 20 50 79
Manager : Mrs Tible

♦ *36 rooms and 2 suites, sound-proofed, with shower or bath, direct dial line and* TV ♦ *Prices : single with shower : 480 F ; double : 550 to 650 F ; suite : 950 F* ♦ *Breakfast with fresh fruit juice, compote and cheese : 35 F* ♦ *Credit cards : American Express, Diners and Visa* ♦ *Facilities : reservations, laundry, dry-cleaning, snacks* ♦ *No dogs allowed* ♦ *Parking facilities : 116 boulevard du Montparnasse* ♦ *Transportation : Metro station Vavin, RER Port-Royal - Buses 68, 82, 83 and 91.*

Mrs Tible loved on sight this hotel built in the 1920s ; she took advantage of it with talent, after several months of hard work.

Now the harmonious design of the entrance shows up, luminous in the soft-pink patina of the walls and the details of a typical architecture : large round-up picture windows, friezes on high square columns, ceilings underlined by pretty geometrical lines. A lounge-bar corner with dark grey armchairs where you'll like to sit under the fan with large quiet blades.

Stylized rooms, very neat, where fabrics and colourful (blue, green, red depending on the floor) accessories liven up the dominant grey. And the bathrooms are ravishing.

But the location at the corner of the boulevards du Montaparnasse and Raspail forces you to keep your windows closed in summer.

Quite reasonnable prices, a generous breakfast : an excellent hotel to which we wish good luck.

Hôtel Lenox - Montparnasse ★★★

15 rue Delambre - 75014 Paris
Tel. : (1) 43 35 34 50 - Telex : 260 745 - Fax : (1) 43 20 46 64
Manager : Mr de Contenson

♦ *52 sound-proofed rooms with shower or bath, direct dial line, TV and safe* ♦ *Bar* ♦ *Prices : single or double : 480 to 570 F ; suite : 850 F* ♦ *Breakfast : 40 F* ♦ *Off-season : January and August* ♦ *Credit cards : American Express, Diners, Eurocard, MasterCard and Visa* ♦ *Facilities : reservations, laundry, dry-cleaning, snacks* ♦ *Dogs allowed* ♦ *Parking facilities : 116 boulevard du Montparnasse* ♦ *Transportation : Metro stations Vavin or Montparnasse, RER Port-Royal - Orly Airport bus : Denfert-Rochereau - Buses 28, 58, 68, 82, 91 and 95.*

The lobby is something more than just pretty, it is refined and gives the key note to this hotel, tastefully renovated. Beautiful period furniture and ancient rugs decorate the entrance hall, further on there is a marble-floored 1930 bar, punctuated by fine supporting columns. Blue doors with varnished wooden frames along the grey corridors. Small but elegant rooms have now a fireplace, now one or two period pieces, now a mirror or a delicate, decorative object. The rooms on the upper storeys are larger and really agreeable. However, all have beautiful white bathrooms tiled at eye level with a bright-coloured edge. The staff is courteous, the clientele, fashionable.

Hôtel de l'Alligator ★★★

39 rue Delambre - 75014 Paris
Tel. : (1) 43 35 18 40 - Telex : 270 545 - Fax : (1) 43 35 30 71
Managers : Mr and Mrs Vic

♦ *35 sound-proofed rooms with shower or bath, direct dial line, TV by satellite and minibar* ♦ *Conference room* ♦ *Prices : single with shower : 370 F, with bath : 470 F ; double : 470 to 520 F ; triple : 570 F* ♦ *Breakfast (buffet) : 30 F* ♦ *Off-season : last 2 weeks of December and August* ♦ *Credit cards : American Express, Diners and Visa* ♦ *Facilities : reservations, laundry, dry-cleaning* ♦ *Dogs allowed* ♦ *Parking facilities : 116 boulevard du Montparnasse* ♦ *Transportation : Metro stations Vavin, Edgar-Quinet or Montparnasse, RER Denfert-Rochereau or Port-Royal - Orly Airport bus : Denfert-Rochereau or avenue du Maine - Buses 28, 58, 68, 82 and 91.*

In this district, animated day and night, this very modern hotel is protected from the street crowd by high quality double windows and by a courtyard on which fifteen of the rooms give.

The lobby is painted light grey, next to it there is a large lounge surmounted by a glass roof filtering the light. Because of this arrangement it looks like an atrium with a gallery running around and leading to a small conference room. The rooms too are grey, a bit small but beautiful (like the bathrooms, tiled light brown or grey) furnished in modern black or light oak.

This is an elegant little hotel designed for a young and modern clientele.

Hôtel Novanox ★★★

155 boulevard du Montparnasse - 75006 Paris
Tel. : (1) 46 33 63 60 - Telex : 201 255 - Fax : (1) 43 26 61 72
Manager : Mr Plasmans

◆ 27 rooms, sound-proofed on the street side, with shower or bath, direct dial line and TV ◆ Bar, conference room ◆ Prices : double with shower or bath : 610 F - Extra bed : 150 F ◆ Breakfast with soft cheese : 40 F ◆ Off-season : December to February ◆ Credit cards : American Express and Visa ◆ Facilities : reservations, laundry, dry-cleaning ◆ Small dogs allowed ◆ Parking facilities : 116 boulevard du Montparnasse ◆ Transportation : Metro stations Vavin, Raspail or Port-Royal, RER Port-Royal - Buses 38, 83 and 91.

New in Montparnasse, Mr Plasmans has made a success.
On the ground floor, Neptune and cherubs fill the prints covering a large folding screen and armchairs, in a harmony of blue and yellow which is original. Parquet floor and light wood in the bar where the 1950s decoration asserts itself.
Definitely well inspired in the choice of his fabrics, the manager has chosen for the rooms beautiful flowered prints and has kept the 1950s atmosphere for the furniture. Small alcoves, good lights. Here are pretty and very comfortable rooms.
In the summer you'll appreciate the quiet side on the rue Notre-Dame-des-Champs on which half of the rooms give.
A completely new hotel with good prospects.

Hôtel Jardin Le Bréa ★★★

**14 rue Bréa - 75006 Paris
Tel. : (1) 43 25 44 41 - Telex : 202 053
Manager : Mrs Painchaud**

♦ *23 rooms with bath, direct dial line,* TV *and minibar* ♦ *Bar and tearoom* ♦ *Prices : single : 490 F ; double : 520 to 650 F ; triple : 620 F* ♦ *Breakfast with orange juice : 40 F* ♦ *Off-season : winter (exclusive of professional shows) and August* ♦ *Credit cards : American Express, Diners and Visa* ♦ *Facilities : reservations, laundry, dry-cleaning, snacks* ♦ *Dogs allowed* ♦ *Parking facilities : 116 boulevard du Montparnasse* ♦ *Transportation : Metro stations Vavin or Montparnasse-Bienvenüe, RER Port-Royal - Buses 47, 68, 82, 83 and 91.*

Near the Luxembourg Gardens, in a still familiar part of Montparnasse, this is a well renovated hotel. The decoration is very personal and obviously it was done with great pleasure. The lobby is bright red enlivened by a lilliputian patio. Mrs Painchaud has created two original pieces of furniture : a writing desk combined with a chest of drawers and an inkstand which can be turned into a card table. These are pretty and practical and you will find them in every room, decorated in a Louis XVI fashion. In the summer, you should stay in one of the twelve back rooms, they are quiet and cool, especially the two large ones in the back house. The small courtyard has charm, plants climb along wooden lattice and the zinc roof-top is painted green. The staff is very careful, in harmony with the house's spirit. A fun hotel (even if some rooms need a new coat of paint) in a district where the atmosphere is that of a village.

Hôtel Danemark ★★★

21 rue Vavin - 75006 Paris
Tel. : (1) 43 26 93 78 - Telex : 202 568 - Fax : (1) 46 34 66 06
Manager : Mrs Nurit

♦ *15 sound-proofed rooms with bath, direct dial line, TV, hair-drier and minibar ; jacuzzi upon request* ♦ *Small conference room* ♦ *Prices : single or double with bath : 520 to 600 F* ♦ *Breakfast with orange juice and cheese : 40 F* ♦ *Off-season : winter (exclusive of professional shows) and August* ♦ *Credit cards : American Express, Diners and Visa* ♦ *Facilities : reservations, laundry, dry-cleaning, snacks* ♦ *Dogs allowed* ♦ *Parking facilities : 116 boulevard du Montparnasse* ♦ *Transportation : Metro stations Vavin or Montparnasse, RER Port-Royal - Buses 58, 68, 75, 82, 83 and 91.*

This used to be a small district establishment which Mr and Mrs Nurit transformed into a splendid hotel art deco. Across the street stands the famous building designed by the architect Sauvage which inspired this hotel's decoration.

The lobby is electric blue, black and white, it is divided into several small sitting rooms with sharp lined, but comfortable furniture. On the back wall the white marble Louis XVI fireplace gives a different touch to this decoration which would otherwise seem too marked.

The same concern about perfection appears in the rooms, furnished in 1930s style showing pleasant lines. Here, it is not the colours but the variety of wooden furniture and doors that makes the difference : oak, light ash wood and mahogany depending on the floor. Between Montparnasse and the Luxembourg Gardens, in a district with a provincial atmosphere, this tiny hotel is a success.

L'Atelier Montparnasse ★★★

49 rue Vavin - 75006 Paris
Tel. : (1) 46 33 60 00 - Fax : (1) 40 51 04 21
Managers : Mr and Mrs Lionel-Dupont

♦ *17 sound-proofed rooms with shower or bath, direct dial line,
TV, hair-drier and minibar* ♦ *Prices : double with shower or
bath : 550 F ; "Fujita" room : 770 F - Extra bed : 100 F*
♦ *Breakfast with orange juice : 40 F* ♦ *Off-season : January and
August* ♦ *Credit cards :American Express, Diners and Visa*
♦ *Facilities : reservations, laundry, dry-cleaning* ♦ *Small dogs
allowed* ♦ *Parking facilities : 116 boulevard du Montparnasse*
♦ *Transportation : Metro stations Notre-Dame-des-Champs or
Montparnasse, RER Port-Royal - Buses 68, 82, 83 and 91.*

An immense flowered mosaic over the floor (a takeoff from the
design of a rug of the Musée des Arts Décoratifs), a superb desk in
burr myrtle, a wall studded with pastiches of paitings from the
beginning of the century : this is quite attracting as the 1930s
decoration perfectly fits in.
Sober, with pastel shades lit up with blue, the rooms are luminous
and agreeable. The surprise comes from the bathrooms : Gauguin,
Picasso, Fujita, Modigliani, Matisse, Chagall, Erté... are evoqued
through molten glass mosaic panels – superb!
Within a stone's throw from the Coupole, an appealing hotel where
the welcome and services are taken on by young and performing
managers.

Villa des Artistes ★★★

9 rue de la Grande-Chaumière - 75006 Paris
Tel. : (1) 43 26 60 86 - Telex : 204 080 - Fax : (1) 43 54 73 70
Managers : Messrs Tourneur

♦ *59 rooms, sound-proofed on the street side, with shower or bath, direct dial line, TV, hair-drier ; trouser-press and minibar in large rooms* ♦ *Patio* ♦ *Prices : single or double with shower : 550 F, with bath : 650 to 750 F - Extra bed : 150 F* ♦ *Continental breakfast or buffet : included* ♦ *Off-season : 15 December to 15 February (exclusive of professional shows) and 15 July to 30 August* ♦ *Credit cards : American Express and Visa* ♦ *Facilities : reservations, laundry, dry-cleaning* ♦ *No dogs allowed* ♦ *Parking facilities : 116 boulevard du Montparnasse* ♦ *Transportation : Metro station Vavin, RER Port-Royal - Buses 58, 68, 82, 83 and 91.*

Coming from the boulevard de Latour-Maubourg, the Tourneur brothers chose for their new address one of Montparnasse's prettiest streets. They transformed an old-fashioned hotel into a 3-star with much personality and a major asset : a large patio leading to a veranda sheltering the cafeteria, and onto which most rooms open (there you can only hear the fountain's murmur)...
Art deco furniture and lights, sienna and dark green are the predominant colours, round leather sofas, fan prints are the characteristics of the ground floor. The rooms are all impeccable and of a good size. Furniture in burr rosewood and covered with fabrics showing blue stripes on a pink background. As for the bathrooms, they are extremely well arranged. And to start a good day, a very generous breakfast-buffet will put everyone in good shape.

Hôtel Ferrandi ★★★

92 rue du Cherche-Midi - 75006 Paris
Tel. : (1) 42 22 97 40 - Telex : 205 201 - Fax : (1) 45 44 89 97
Manager : Mrs Lafond

◆ *41 rooms and 1 suite, sound-proofed, with shower or bath, direct dial line, TV, hair-drier* ◆ *Garage* ◆ *Prices : single or double with shower : 385 F, with bath : 500 to 850 F ; suite : 950 to 1 200 F* ◆ *Breakfast with fresh fruit juice and homemade jams : 50 F* ◆ *Off-season : July and August* ◆ *Credit cards : American Express, Diners, JCB and Visa* ◆ *Facilities : reservations, laundry, dry-cleaning, snacks* ◆ *Dogs allowed* ◆ *Parking facilities : in the hotel and Bon Marché car park* ◆ *Transportation : Metro stations Saint-Placide or Sèvres-Babylone - Buses 39, 48, 84 89, 94, 95 and 96.*

On a street bordered by small shops, Parisian cafés, antic shops and workshops in courtyards, the Hôtel Ferrandi offers, behind its white shutters, a decoration in accordance with the building's style, Restauration. The staircase with its light handrail displays a trompe-l'œil of yellow and ginger-coloured marble. The lounge is beautiful and comfortable with its fireplace and mahogany furniture, the damask curtains with pink, soft-green and plum-coloured stripes sing over the light-green patina of the walls. The breakfast room opens on the lattice work of a window box and the paved courtyard. Everything is up to it : the welcome could not be nicer ; the fruit juices – fresh ; the room decoration (our favorites : four large rooms with two windows – numbers ending with 3 – and the singles, those ending with 8. Tester beds, Polish canopies or brass beds, alcoves, polished cupboards, fireplaces of white marble, Liberty print or curtains with a leafy pattern, white bedspreads. A lot of blue also. It is absolutely charming, even the bathrooms, tiled in white or covered with ginger-coloured marble.

Hôtel Sainte-Beuve ★★★

9 rue Sainte-Beuve - 75006 Paris
Tel. : (1) 45 48 20 07 - Telex : 270 182 - Fax : (1) 45 48 67 52
Manager : Mrs Compagnon

♦ *23 rooms with bath, direct dial line, TV, safe and minibar* ♦ *Bar* ♦ *Prices : single or double : 650 to 1 100 F ; suite : 1 400 F ; apt. : 1 550 F* ♦ *Breakfast : 70 F* ♦ *Off-season : winter (exclusive of professional shows) and August* ♦ *Credit cards : American Express and Visa* ♦ *Facilities : reservations, laundry, dry-cleaning, snacks* ♦ *No dogs allowed* ♦ *Parking facilities : 116 boulevard du Montparnasse* ♦ *Transportation : Metro stations Vavin or Notre-Dame-des-Champs, RER Port-Royal - Buses 68, 82, 83 and 91.*

The rue Sainte-Beuve is a very quiet passage between the nearby Luxembourg Gardens and the animated boulevard du Montparnasse. The location is ideal for this magnificently renovated hotel : antique columns, long white curtains, carpets of faded colours compose a neo-classic decoration softened by the marble of the fireplace. There the hotel's guests sit and mingle with visitors from the outside who are attracted by the sumptuous breakfast : croissants from Mulot (a famous bakery) and jams from the convent of the Solitude des Sœurs d'Ivry.

A model for harmonies in soft shades (yellow, pink, cream), such are the rooms where ancient furnishing and beautiful prints add a touch of warmth. On the fifth and sixth floors (with sloping ceilings) they are really large and extremely comfortable. The very refined bathrooms are decorated in pale colours. Night and day room-service, and a careful welcome make this a "grand hôtel".

Hôtel Sèvres-Azur ★★

22 rue de l'Abbé-Grégoire - 75006 Paris
Tel. : (1) 45 48 84 07 - Telex : 205 847
Managers : Mr and Mrs Jolin

♦ *31 sound-proofed rooms with bath, direct dial line,* TV, *hair-drier*
♦ *Prices : single or double : 370 to 420 F ; triple : 420 to 480 F*
♦ *Breakfast : 25 F* ♦ *Off-season : January* ♦ *Credit cards :*
American Express, Diners and Visa ♦ *Facilities : reservations,*
laundry, dry-cleaning ♦ *Dogs allowed* ♦ *Parking facilities : Bon*
Marché car park and rue Velpeau ♦ *Transportation : Metro*
stations Saint-Placide or Sèvres-Babylone - Buses 39, 48, 70, 87,
89, 94, 95 and 96.

Look at the balconies. They were built in 1880, gorgeous, with
balusters of wrought iron, they are round and form hanging window
boxes ; and they dress up the façade of a new 2-star as welcoming
and comfortable as a 3-star, an excellent address.
Once through the door, nothing reminds of the façade. Mr and
Mrs Jolin have arranged an elegant and modern lobby, playing
exclusively with lines and materials in order to highlight the space.
Superb veneer underlined by long, thin black lines, flooring of large,
light-grey tiles, light-coloured walls. A small red and black lounge ;
a breakfast room in a gradation from grey to black. In the back,
bamboo and roses in a tiny courtyard. The street is quiet ; the
backyard, large and bright. Decorated in the same fashion, the
rooms are of a nice size, the walls are pale pink enlightened by a
brick red section at the bedhead, grey moquette, flowered cotton
fabrics. Many brass beds. Extra pieces of furniture and well
designed linen cupboards. Impeccable bathrooms where the
imposing round washstands have large edges.

Hôtel Le Saint-Grégoire ★★★

43 rue de l'Abbé-Grégoire - 75006 Paris
Tel. : (1) 45 48 23 23 - Telex : 205 343 - Fax : (1) 45 48 33 95
Managers : Mrs Agaud and Mr Bouvier

♦ *20 sound-proofed rooms with bath (1 with shower), direct dial line, TV, hair-drier* ♦ *Prices : double : 650 to 1 100 F ; suite and room with terrace : 1 100 F - Extra bed : 100 F* ♦ *Breakfast with fresh fruit juice : 55 F* ♦ *Off-season : winter (exclusive of professional shows) and August* ♦ *Credit cards : American Express, Diners, Eurocard, MasterCard and Visa* ♦ *Facilities : reservations, laundry, dry-cleaning, snacks* ♦ *Small dogs allowed* ♦ *Parking facilities : rue de Rennes, opposite the* FNAC ♦ *Transportation : Metro station Saint-Placide - Buses 48, 89, 94, 95 and 96.*

New in Montparnasse, the Saint-Grégoire is a hotel which will soon become famous. The interior decoration shows the right combination of fashionable neo-classic and Anglo-Saxon styles to be at the same time beautiful and comfortable. In the hallway, the colours are subtle and warm ; the reading room is brightened by a tiny green patio and on both sides of an exquisite fireplace are two sofas. When it is cold outside, a log fire usually warms up the room. The rooms are spacious and this has allowed a harmonious disposition where each piece of furniture has its place. They are furnished in 19th century style and everything has character, the white quilted bedspreads, the pale-pink flooring and brown marble adding a touch of warmth to the bathrooms, all this shows to what extent the decoration was thought out. In summer, ask for a room with a terrace. This hotel is a bit isolated but is well worth going out of your way.

Hôtel Beauvoir ★★

43 avenue Georges-Bernanos - 75005 Paris
Tel. : (1) 43 25 57 10 - Telex : 250 942 - Fax : (1) 43 54 31 87
Manager : Mr Atmoun

◆ *29 rooms with shower or bath, direct dial line and TV* ◆ *Pool room* ◆ *Prices : single : 290 F ; double : 380 to 465 F - Extra bed : 50 F* ◆ *Breakfast with orange juice : 29 F* ◆ *No off-season* ◆ *Credit cards : American Express, Eurocard, MasterCard and Visa* ◆ *Facilities : reservations, laundry, dry-cleaning* ◆ *Dogs allowed* ◆ *Parking facilities : 116 boulevard du Montparnasse* ◆ *Transportation : Metro station and RER Port-Royal - Buses 38, 83 and 91.*

Opposite the restaurant "La Closerie des Lilas", meeting place of the Latin Quarter and Montparnasse, the six-floor-high Hôtel Beauvoir overlooks the Observatoire gardens which end almost at its doorstep. This outstanding location deserved that this old local hotel went to some trouble of renovation. It has now begun : warm atmosphere in the lounge lined with ginger-coloured buckskin, with beams and half-timbering, oriental rugs and wall mirrors. The rooms are well designed, not very large but bright, they are a nice place to live in since they got a new coat of paint. Light-pink or beige walls, dark bamboo or wooden contemporary furniture, brown tiles with small flowers in the bathrooms. We liked best the pretty singles and the two rooms on the sixth floor with a view leading, over the Paris roofs, to the hill of Chaillot… And the pool room arranged in the basement.

Hôtel Observatoire-Luxembourg ★★★

107 boulevard Saint-Michel - 75005 Paris
Tel. : (1) 46 34 10 12 - Telex : 200 456 - Fax : (1) 46 33 73 86
Manager : Mr Bonneau

♦ *37 sound-proofed rooms with shower or bath, direct dial line,* TV *and safe* ♦ *Conference room* ♦ *Prices : single : 500 to 660 F ; double : 630 to 770 F ; triple : 770 to 900 F - Extra bed : 100 F* ♦ *Breakfast with orange juice and cheese : 35 F* ♦ *Off-season : winter (exclusive of professional shows)* ♦ *Credit cards : American Express, Diners, Eurocard, JCB, MasterCard and Visa* ♦ *Facilities : reservations, laundry, dry-cleaning, snacks* ♦ *No dogs allowed* ♦ *Parking facilities : 20 rue Soufflot* ♦ *Transportation : RER Luxembourg - Buses 21, 27, 38, 82 and 84.*

Almost at the corner of the Luxembourg Gardens, this hotel is at the limit between the boulevard Saint-Michel and a district where reigns a provincial tranquility. Out of the windows, a lot of light and a view over trees, either along the boulevard, the Luxembourg or the garden of the Institut des Jeunes-Sourds. Closeby, the bells of Saint-Jacques-du-Haut-Pas happily mark out the hours. In this 3-star hotel the welcome is sweet, the decoration new and warm : a ginger-coloured, beige and brown monochrome, even in the rooms Louis-Philippe style. The starting point is a quite extraordinary marble. It was used for the floor in the lobby and in the dining room it also glitters on the square tabletops, under the thin fitment of the low-tension lamps... In the living room, a cosy sofa corner with touches of old rose ; the bathrooms are a grey universe of marble ; some rooms are yellow, others soft blue or peacock blue... Choose rooms whose numbers end with 6 or 7, they have view on the Luxembourg, or with 3, 4, or 5, from the second floor up, they look out on the garden of the Institut des Jeunes-Sourds and further you'll see the dome of the Val-de-Grâce.

Hôtel de l'Abbaye St-Germain ★★★

10 rue Cassette - 75006 Paris
Tel. : (1) 45 44 38 11 - Fax : (1) 45 48 07 86
Manager : Mr Lafortune

♦ *44 rooms and 4 duplex apt. (with terrace, TV and minibar) with bath, direct dial line, (TV in large rooms)* ♦ *Patio, bar* ♦ *Prices : double : 690 to 1 200 F ; suite : 1 500 to 1 800 F - Extra bed : 250 F* ♦ *Breakfast included* ♦ *Off-season : winter (exclusive of professional shows) and August* ♦ *No credit cards accepted* ♦ *Facilities : reservations, laundry, dry-cleaning, snacks* ♦ *No dogs allowed* ♦ *Parking facilities : place Saint-Sulpice* ♦ *Transportation : Metro stations Saint-Sulpice, Rennes or Sèvres-Babylone - Buses 48, 63, 70, 84, 87, 95 and 96.*

It is difficult to resist the charm of this beautiful hotel enclosed between a courtyard and a garden and so near the Luxembourg Gardens.

The very attractive decoration is composed of two large sitting rooms following one another, marble flooring, some antique furniture and beautiful sofas next to a fireplace. Further on there is a vast patio, its walls are overlayed with lattice work. The rooms are just as refined. The colours of the walls (blue or beige) are in harmony with the ornamental mouldings around the door frames (brick, greyish blue, yellow) and the fabrics. The 19th century furnishing goes well with the brass or bamboo frames of the beds. The pretty bathrooms are tiled in marble. Conscious that the rooms are relatively small, except those on the garden level, the management has recently opened four duplex apartments and one large room on the third floor. Do not forget this address, the hotel is located in an almost provincial district.

Hôtel Perreyve ★★

63 rue Madame - 75006 Paris
Tel. : (1) 45 48 35 01 - Telex : 205 080 - Fax : (1) 42 84 03 30
Manager : Mr Doumergue

♦ *30 rooms with shower or bath, direct dial line and TV* ♦ *Prices :
single : 378 to 428 F ; double : 406 to 456 F ; triple : 644 F - Extra
bed : 160 F* ♦ *Breakfast included* ♦ *Off-season : January,
February and August* ♦ *Credit cards : American Express, Diners
and Visa* ♦ *Facilities : reservations, laundry, dry-cleaning* ♦ *No
dogs allowed* ♦ *Parking facilities : place Saint-Sulpice*
♦ *Transportation : Metro station Rennes - Buses 27, 58, 82, 83, 84
and 89.*

This unpretentious hotel is located between Montparnasse and
Saint-Germain-des-Prés, two minutes away from the Luxembourg
Gardens, its clientele is composed mostly of scholars and doctors
who take pleasure in the quietness of the rue Madame.
An awning over the main entrance, mosaic paving and stained glass
windows along the stairway were kept from the original house, built
at the beginning of the century. The colours chosen for the
comfortable and simple sitting room are blue and brown.
Half the rooms have just been renovated : pale pink walls with
matching flowered curtains and a frieze. Elsewhere, on the fourth
floor, almond-green wallpaper, pink curtains and pink or white
bedspreads. The bathrooms are modern and clean. We prefer the
corner rooms with two windows or those on the sixth floor, the
ceilings do not slope but the view on the surrounding terraces is
amusing. Simple and peaceful this is a nice hotel with moderate
tariffs.

Hôtel Récamier ★★

3 bis place Saint-Sulpice - 75006 Paris
Tel. : (1) 43 26 04 89
Manager : Mr Dauphin

♦ *30 rooms with washbasins, shower or bath, direct dial line*
♦ *Prices : single : 380 to 450 F ; double : 410 to 480 F ; suite :*
700 F - Extra bed : 120 F ♦ *Breakfast : 30 F* ♦ *Off-season :*
winter (exclusive of professional shows) ♦ *No credit cards*
accepted ♦ *Facilities : reservations* ♦ *No dogs allowed* ♦ *Parking*
facilities : place Saint-Sulpice ♦ *Transportation : Metro stations*
Saint-Sulpice, Saint-Germain-des-Prés or Mabillon - Buses 58, 63,
70, 84, 86, 87 and 96.

The imposing Saint-Sulpice church has marked this quite empty
square, where, most of the time, you'll only hear birds, children and
water flowing from the fountain. Here, although Saint-Germain-des-
Prés is nearby, it is the province and the Récamier was meant for
this place.

The decoration is old-fashioned : wallpaper with a large flower
pattern, green plants and a mirror in the entrance hall. Peacefully
lying on top of the reception desk, the house cat keeps an eye on
things, which are not supposed to ever change.

In the quite large and nicely furnished rooms, the wallpaper also
creates the atmosphere : small flower pattern, which the
management will replace by the identical as soon as it shows the
slightest damage. This imparts an old-fashioned and charming air to
the rooms. The prettiest have a double exposure, they give on the
square and the sunny courtyard. As for those with washbasins only,
they overlook the square and are wonderful if you like to observe
the life going on in the neighbourhood.

Hôtel de l'Odéon ★★★

13 rue Saint-Sulpice - 75006 Paris
Tel. : (1) 43 25 70 11 - Telex : 206 731 - Fax : (1) 43 29 97 34
Managers : Mr and Mrs Pilfert

♦ *30 rooms, sound-proofed on the street side (air-conditioning in some rooms), with shower or bath, direct dial line, cable TV, hairdrier and safe* ♦ *Prices : single : 490 to 590 F ; double : 620 to 720 F ; triple : 800 F - Extra bed : 100 F* ♦ *Breakfast : 39 F* ♦ *Off-season : December* ♦ *Credit cards : American Express, Diners, Eurocard, MasterCard and Visa* ♦ *Facilities : reservations, laundry, dry-cleaning, snacks* ♦ *Dogs allowed* ♦ *Parking facilities : place Saint-Sulpice and opposite 21 rue de l'Ecole-de-Médecine* ♦ *Transportation : Metro stations Odéon, Saint-Sulpice or Saint-Germain, RER Cluny-Saint-Michel - Buses 58, 63, 70, 86, 87 and 96.*

Protected by its double windows and giving on a courtyard, this hotel is absolutely silent, although it is located in a very busy street. Just like all the old houses in this area, it still has beams and stone walls which were used as a background for a nice decoration showing a strange combination of Medieval and Régence styles.
The rooms are a surprise : almost all of them are furnished with the most extraordinary beds, the frames are in cast iron, painted sheet iron with a pearly coating or brass with rococo volutes, there are canopy beds or beds as high as they used to be a long time ago. Finds showing a lot of humour, mottled with patience, kitsch bedspreads in white lace all this creates a surprising decoration. It is now your turn to discover it.

Relais Saint-Germain ★★★

9 carrefour de l'Odéon - 75006 Paris
Tel. : (1) 43 29 12 05 - Telex : 201 889 - Fax : (1) 46 33 45 30
Manager : Mr Laipsker

♦ *17 rooms with bath, direct dial line, cable TV, hair-drier, safe and minibar* ♦ *Prices : single : 1 160 F ; double : 1 320 F ; suite : 1 760 F* ♦ *Breakfast with fruit, cheese and cereals : included* ♦ *No off-season* ♦ *Credit cards : American Express, Diners and Visa* ♦ *Facilities : reservations, laundry, dry-cleaning, snacks* ♦ *Dogs allowed* ♦ *Parking facilities : place Saint-Sulpice and opposite 21 rue de l'Ecole-de-Médecine* ♦ *Transportation : Metro station Odéon, RER Cluny-Saint-Michel - Buses 58, 63, 70, 86, 87 and 96.*

A little isolated from the carrefour de l'Odéon, this tiny hotel is caught between two old houses, and protected by a glass wall closed by a bluish green door. Inside reign silence and beauty. Elegant antique furniture, 18th century French landscapes elegantly framed are reflected in the mirror wall of the small, bright-pink sitting room. A picture window now opens on the breakfast room, taken on from a neighbouring shop, and it is a great success with pink silk ruffles, exotic armchairs and tablecloths showing elaborate prints. All the bedrooms are different, beautiful and spacious. The prints, colours, period chests of drawers, decorative objects, desk lamps, even the round shaped bouquets in the flower stands, were chosen with infinite care. The suite on the top floor is a wonder : yellow and periwinkle blue, vast and luminous with several beams.
Obviously, welcome and service are perfect here. This miniature is really a high quality hotel.

Grand Hôtel des Balcons ★★

3 rue Casimir-Delavigne - 75006 Paris
Tel. : (1) 46 34 78 50 - Fax : (1) 46 34 06 27
Manager : Mr and Mrs Corroyer

♦ *55 rooms, sound-proofed on the street side, with shower or bath, direct dial line and TV* ♦ *Prices : single or double : 280 to 350 F ; triple : 450 F* ♦ *Breakfast with orange juice and cheese : 40 F* ♦ *No off-season* ♦ *Credit cards : MasterCard and Visa* ♦ *Facilities : reservations* ♦ *Dogs allowed* ♦ *Parking facilities : 20 rue Soufflot and opposite 21 rue de l'Ecole-de-Médecine* ♦ *Transportation : Metro station Odéon, RER Luxembourg - Buses 21, 27, 38, 58, 63, 82, 84, 85 and 89.*

Not far away from the Luxembourg Gardens, in one of those pretty streets going toward the boulevard Saint-Germain, this hotel has beautiful balconies.

Inside, in the lobby and along the stairway there are stained glass windows made at the beginning of the century. This has certainly inspired the renovation of the woodworks on the ground floor and particularly that of the main entrance door. But it is furnished in different styles (Louis XV, 1900s, rustic...) which create a funny, comfortable and unpretentious arrangement. The last touch to this decoration are palm trees and a collection of green plants.

In the rooms the decoration is more simple, they are papered in pink, red, green or blue, with net curtains and small lampshades to soften the light.

However what's best is the welcome : a friendly spontaneity creating a very pleasant atmosphere.

Hôtel Luxembourg ★★★

4 rue de Vaugirard - 75006 Paris
Tel. : (1) 43 25 35 90 - Telex : 270 879 - Fax : (1) 43 26 60 84
Manager : Mr Mesenge

♦ *34 rooms with bath, direct dial line, TV, hair-drier and minibar* ♦ *Flowered courtyard* ♦ *Prices : single or double : 565 F ; triple : 685 F* ♦ *Breakfast (buffet) : 40 F* ♦ *Off-season : 15 December to March and August* ♦ *Credit cards : American Express, Diners and Visa* ♦ *Facilities : reservations, laundry, dry-cleaning* ♦ *Dogs allowed* ♦ *Parking facilities : 20 rue Soufflot and rue de l'Ecole-de-Médecine* ♦ *Transportation : Metro station Odéon, RER Luxembourg or Cluny-Saint-Michel - Buses 21, 27, 38, 58, 63, 82, 84, 85, 86, 87, 89 and 96.*

The hotel has a new manager, but it kept a charm which is not often found. Completely new lobby, lined with blue buckskin, leading to a lounge-bar where a chest of camphor wood and beautiful sea charts show the management's passion for sea voyages. White courtyard, planted with ivy and balsamine. The rooms, be it on the courtyard or the street side, are large enough, light with now plain, now striped walls, and furnished in lead-white wood Louis XVI style. Good wardrobes and nice little bathrooms.

The breakfast room, vaulted as many others in Paris, has one characteristic : it still has an imposing pillar, remains of the Philippe-Auguste city walls. An extremely friendly hotel with quite reasonnable prices.

Hôtel Sénateur ★★★

10 rue de Vaugirard - 75006 Paris
Tel. : (1) 43 26 08 83 - Telex : 200 091 - Fax : (1) 46 34 04 66
Manager : Mrs Chertier

♦ *43 rooms with shower or bath, direct dial line, TV, hair-drier, safe and minibar* ♦ *Conference room* ♦ *Prices : single : 580 F ; double : 680 F ; suite : 1 080 F - Extra bed : 100 F* ♦ *Breakfast with orange juice : 39 F* ♦ *Off-season : winter, July and August* ♦ *Credit cards : American Express, Diners and Visa* ♦ *Facilities : reservations, laundry, dry-cleaning* ♦ *Dogs allowed* ♦ *Parking facilities : 20 rue Soufflot and opposite 21 rue de l'Ecole-de-Médecine* ♦ *Transportation : Metro station Odéon, RER Luxembourg or Cluny-Saint-Michel - Buses 21, 27, 38, 58, 82, 84, 85 and 89.*

Right next door to the Luxembourg Gardens and the Théâtre de l'Odéon, this hotel is all new. The modern lobby in light oak woodwork and sandstone flooring is welcoming ; a flowered light well brightens it. In the lounge, a tropical landscape was painted on one of the walls, green 1930s armchairs and exotic plants impart a warm gaiety. The basement is occupied by a conference room equipped with all that is necessary and a large and light breakfast room. Curiously, the decoration does not show as much warmth in the bedrooms, too functional maybe. If possible, stay in the rooms bearing numbers in 2 or 3, they are larger ; else, choose a duplex apartment with a very agreeable sitting room corner. Beautiful bathrooms, also grey, with polished granit around the washbasins. A hotel which, little by little, finds the right note.

Hôtel Latitudes Saint-Germain ★★★

7-11 rue Saint-Benoît - 75006 Paris
Tel. : (1) 42 61 53 53 - Telex : 213 531 - Fax : (1) 49 27 09 33
Manager : Mrs Guiné

♦ *117 rooms, sound-proofed and air-conditioned, with bath, direct dial line, TV by satellite and video, hair-drier and minibar* ♦ *Pianobar* ♦ *Prices : single : 750 F ; double : 840 F - Extra bed : 200 F* ♦ *Breakfast with orange juice, yogurt, cheese and fruit : 55 F* ♦ *Off-season : winter (exclusive of professional shows) and August* ♦ *Credit cards : American Express, Diners, Eurocard, MasterCard and Visa* ♦ *Facilities : reservations, laundry, dry-cleaning, snacks* ♦ *Small dogs allowed* ♦ *Parking facilities : opposite 169 boulevard Saint-Germain* ♦ *Transportation : Metro station Saint-Germain-des-Prés - Buses 39, 48, 63, 70, 86, 87 and 95.*

This is the best location for people who love Paris ; a quite discreet setting for lovers of the area ; a number of rooms allowing hope even at the height of the season : the chain Latitudes has made a success out of this first Parisian hotel… Space and light, materials and shades pertain an airy atmosphere to the lounge. Next to it, a grey and silver living room ; at the back, under a glass roof, the breakfast room where a fresco represents the ancient door to an abbey. A wide staircase goes down to the bar which becomes animated in the evening with the piano, and during the weekends with jazz concerts. Only colour marks a difference between the rooms : light green on the first floor, salmon pink on the second, intense blue on the third and pink on the fourth… Ceruse grey furniture of Directoire style, wardrobes with mirrors, cotton fabrics give some elegance to this standard decor. The rooms whose number ends with 6 or 7 overlook the church tower (they also communicate) ; those ending with 14 or 15 have three windows overlooking the rue Saint-Benoît. In the summer choose the courtyard side!

Crystal Hôtel ★★

24 rue Saint-Benoît - 75006 Paris
Tel. : (1) 45 48 85 14 - Telex : 201 021 - Fax : (1) 45 49 16 45
Manager : Mrs Choukroun

♦ *26 rooms, sound-proofed, with shower or bath, direct dial line,* TV *and minibar* ♦ *Prices : single with shower : 350 F ; double with bath : 600 F ; suite : 900 F - Extra bed : 100 F* ♦ *Breakfast with fresh fruit juice : 35 F* ♦ *Off-season : winter (exclusive of professional shows) and August* ♦ *Credit cards : American Express, Diners and Visa* ♦ *Facilities : reservations, laundry, dry-cleaning* ♦ *Dogs allowed* ♦ *Parking facilities : opposite 169 boulevard Saint-Germain* ♦ *Transportation : Metro station Saint-Germain-des-Prés - Buses 39, 48, 58, 63, 70, 86, 87, 95 and 96.*

This hotel, attractive on sight, is rooted to the heart of the Saint-Germain-des-Prés where Boris Vian, Sartre and Gréco used to meet. A friendly and tonic atmosphere prevails as the cosmopolitan clientele of intellectuals is very faithful.

An awning and two beautiful lanterns mark the entrance way. In the cosy and welcoming lobby, you'll see two large and worn out Chesterfield sofas, a narrow sideboard with twisted legs and a reception desk made of heavy wood.

The rooms are just as we like them : never small, furnished with taste in 19th century English style, papered with flowered wallpaper matching the fabric of the curtains ; otherwise, they are painted in soft colours enhanced by pretty cotton fabrics. The bathrooms are neat and modern. This hotel has a lot of character and its tariffs are still reasonnable.

Hôtel Saint-Germain-des-Prés ★★★

36 rue Bonaparte - 75006 Paris
Tel. : (1) 43 26 00 19 - Telex : 200 409 - Fax : (1) 40 46 83 63
Managers : Mr and Mrs Le Boudec

♦ *28 rooms and 2 suites, sound-proofed on the street side, with shower or bath, direct dial line, TV, hair-drier, safe and minibar* ♦ *Bar* ♦ *Prices : single : 650 F ; double : 700 F ; triple : 1 200 F ; suite : 1 500 F - Extra bed : 200 F* ♦ *Breakfast with cheese and prunes : 50 F* ♦ *Off-season : winter (exclusive of professional shows) and August* ♦ *Credit card : Visa* ♦ *Facilities : reservations, laundry, dry-cleaning* ♦ *No dogs allowed* ♦ *Parking facilities : opposite 169 boulevard Saint-Germain* ♦ *Transportation : Metro station Saint-Germain-des-Prés, RER Cluny-Saint-Michel or Gare d'Orsay - Buses 27, 39, 48, 63, 70, 86, 87, 95 and 96.*

When you are on the place Saint-Germain, the rue Bonaparte is at the junction between two districts : the publishers' district and that of antique dealers. This hotel is located next to Paris oldest bell tower, and is very much liked abroad.

The dark red velvet draperies are sumptuous and theatrical, they separate the entrance from the lounge. Period chairs and large leather sofas give a warm atmosphere to this large room. In the back there is a wall behind glass, it is brightly lit and in summer, abundantly flowered. Corridors designed in trompe-l'œil are extremely decorative. Little panels representing a comedy scene or a landscape were hung on each door. The rooms are no less interesting : beams, flowered tapestries, stained glass windows, woodwork, canopy bed (in room #26), and of course, marble bathrooms. On the whole, this quite heavy decoration is well done. However don't stay in the front rooms in the summertime, because the rue Bonaparte is a busy street.

Hôtel de Fleurie ★★★

32 rue Grégoire-de-Tours - 75006 Paris
Tel. : (1) 43 29 59 81 - Telex : 206 153 - Fax : (1) 43 29 68 44
Manager : Mr Marolleau

♦ *29 sound-proofed rooms with shower or bath, direct dial line, cable TV, hair-drier, towel-warmer, safe and minibar* ♦ *Prices : single : 500 F ; double : 650 to 850 F ; triple : 1 000 F - Extra bed : 150 F* ♦ *Breakfast with fresh fruit juice, cheese and fruit : 40 F* ♦ *Off-season : 15 November to 15 December and August* ♦ *Credit cards : American Express, Diners, Eurocard, JCB, MasterCard and Visa* ♦ *Facilities : reservations, laundry, dry-cleaning, snacks* ♦ *No dogs allowed* ♦ *Parking facilities : opposite 21 rue de l'Ecole-de-Médecine* ♦ *Transportation : Metro station Odéon, RER Cluny-Saint-Michel or Luxembourg - Buses 58, 63, 70, 86, 87 and 96.*

A very white façade, with niches sheltering little statues, brightens up this ignored passageway near the place de l'Odéon. The hotel has been recently renovated. Thanks to the taste for details, the talent and also to the sense of welcome of Mr and Mrs Marolleau, it is a success. The hallway is tiled in baked clay, woodworks and pots of greenery give fresshness to the ground floor. The living room is decorated in Régence style, with a little Chesterfield sofa, an inlaid chest of drawers among soft pink woodworks and a brick and stone wall. The result is a feeling of true conviviality... Just as agreeable, sound-proofed, of a nice size, the rooms show a game of light shades and delicate prints. (Our favorites ? rooms #60 and #61 in the attic, and the large rooms bearing numbers in 4.) A pretty piece of furniture, a bouquet, a watercolour, perfectly white bedspreads, all this adds a personal touch to the decoration. In the marble bathrooms, nothing is missing, not even towel-warmers !

Hôtel La Louisiane ★★

60 rue de Seine - 75006 Paris
Tel. : (1) 43 29 59 30 - Fax : (1) 46 34 23 87
Manager : Mr Blanchot

♦ *79 rooms, sound-proofed on the street side, with shower or bath, direct dial line ♦ Prices : single or double with shower : 350 to 500 F ; single or double with bath : 550 to 600 F ♦ Breakfast with orange juice : included ♦ Off-season : winter (exclusive of professional shows) ♦ Credit cards : Diners and Visa ♦ Facilities : reservations ♦ No dogs allowed ♦ Parking facilities : 27 rue Mazarine and opposite 169 boulevard Saint-Germain ♦ Transportation : Metro stations Mabillon or Saint-Germain-des-Prés - Buses 58, 63, 70, 86, 87 and 96.*

The Hôtel La Louisiane is an integrant part of the Saint-Germain district. Amidst flower and vegetable shops, it pursues steadily, in the middle of the rue de Buci market, its career of a typically French hotel, so dear to the dreams of Americans visiting Paris.

The building's white façade, the big black letters of a 1930s graphism, carpets and a handrail art deco style beautifully mark this hotel with an apparently unchanging style. A small corridor leads to a tiny sitting room and to an austere dining room. Along white corridors are the newly painted rooms. They are often small (except for three large ones with a rounded wall), but practical, the bathrooms are correct and clean.

Nothing very attractive on sight, not even the prices but a simplicity with no false pretense, an original and nice welcome give some charm to this hotel where you will come back.

Hôtel Les Marronniers ★★★

21 rue Jacob - 75006 Paris
Tel. : (1) 43 25 30 60 - Fax : (1) 40 46 83 56
Manager : Mr Henneveux

♦ *37 rooms with shower or bath (4 large ones for 3 to 4 people)*
♦ *Garden* ♦ *Prices : single : 420 F ; double : 585 to 650 F ; large room : 920 and 1 070 F - Extra bed : 120 F* ♦ *Breakfast : 42 F*
♦ *No credit cards accepted* ♦ *Facilities : reservations* ♦ *No dogs allowed* ♦ *Parking facilities : opposite 169 boulevard Saint-Germain and place Saint-Sulpice* ♦ *Transportation : Metro station Saint-Germain-des-Prés - Buses 39, 48, 63, 68, 69, 86, 87 and 95.*

The name is pretty, the location between garden and courtyard is exceptional. There is an elegant veranda in a Napoleon III style, where ruffled curtains, strewn with tiny bouquets of flowers, filter the light. This is a refuge to have breakfast, read or have a drink. A real garden shaded by beautiful trees and something new in the service : the receptionist is smiling and the yellow, pink and green carpet found its way to every floor. The wallpaper in the rooms is now light-coloured. The furnishing is dark and so heavy that even the beams and the Louis XIII chairs do not alleviate all this. The bathrooms are clean, but neither very large, nor very modern. Stay on the first three floors, in a room whose number ends with 1 or 2 (they give on the garden, the others face a wall), or from the fourth floor up, in a room on the garden side from which you'll see the Saint-Germain-des-Prés bell tower and the roofs of Paris. As for the side giving on the courtyard, stay in the fifth or sixth floor rooms with sloping ceilings and a view on the roofs. A hotel we like a lot.

Hôtel des Deux Continents ★★

25 rue Jacob - 75006 Paris
Tel. : (1) 43 26 72 46
Manager : Mrs Chresteil

♦ *40 rooms with shower or bath, direct dial line and TV by satellite*
♦ *Prices : single with shower or bath : 380 to 500 F ; double with shower or bath : 450 to 600 F - Extra bed : 150 F* ♦ *Breakfast included* ♦ *No off-season* ♦ *Credit cards : Diners, Eurocard, MasterCard and Visa* ♦ *Facilities : reservations* ♦ *No dogs allowed* ♦ *Parking facilities : opposite 169 boulevard Saint-Germain and place Saint-Sulpice* ♦ *Transportation : Metro station Saint-Germain-des-Prés, RER Gare d'Orsay - Buses 24, 27, 39, 48, 63, 70, 86, 87, 95 and 96.*

This is a nice hotel to live in. It has a charming simplicity and a peaceful atmosphere. Under the low ceiling, you feel cosy in the 19th century furnishing. The welcome is delightful : the family who manages this hotel for many generations now, shares its taste for languages with the staff, they have even started to learn Japanese and Esperanto in order to tell people what to visit in their area. The rooms are quite big and well arranged and you'll pay the cheapest possible rates for this district. More than half of the rooms are settled in two small houses without a lift, located between two small courtyards newly painted where balsamines bloom when the time comes. Sloping ceilings for the back rooms on the top floors, beams and a balcony for the front rooms on the sixth floor. All of them are decorated with a refined simplicity : flower-patterned wallpaper, beige, green or mustard moquette, white quilted bedspreads, curtain rods in copper or painted wood and bathrooms shaped just like this irregular old house.

Hôtel d'Angleterre ★★★

44 rue Jacob - 75006 Paris
Tel. : (1) 42 60 34 72 - Fax : (1) 42 60 16 93
Manager : Mrs Soumier

♦ *29 rooms with bath, direct dial line and* TV ♦ *Patio* ♦ *Prices : single : 700 F ; double : 850 to 950 F - Extra bed : + 30%* ♦ *Breakfast with orange juice : 30 F* ♦ *No off-season* ♦ *Credit cards : American Express, Diners and Visa* ♦ *Facilities : reservations, laundry, dry-cleaning* ♦ *No dogs allowed* ♦ *Parking facilities : opposite 169 boulevard Saint-Germain* ♦ *Transportation : Metro station Saint-Germain-des-Prés - Buses 39, 48, 63, 70, 86, 87, 95 and 96.*

The classic decoration is a success, the patio, a delight, most of the rooms open onto it and the bar is there. All this adds charm to this perfect hotel.

The ancient staircase shows a fine marble trompe-l'œil and the handrail is beautiful. It leads to ravishing rooms, all different, where wistaria, plants, mirrors, Venitian chandeliers and beautiful furnishing abound. Remember the suites and the very large rooms on the garden side. Why did they redo four rooms at the back of the patio ? Curiously, now that they have become suites, thanks to a wall folding screen, they have lost their beautiful proportions. Apart from this little faulse note, this hotel, managed with energy and remarkably silent is one of Paris best place to stay.

Hôtel Madison ★★★

143 boulevard Saint-Germain - 75006 Paris
Tel. : (1) 43 29 72 50 - Telex : 201 628 - Fax : (1) 43 29 72 50
Manager : Mr Hurand

♦ *55 rooms, sound-proofed and air-conditioned, with shower or bath, direct dial line, TV and minibar* ♦ *Bar* ♦ *Prices : single : 630 to 730 F ; double : 890 to 1 090 F - Extra bed : 210 F* ♦ *Breakfast included* ♦ *Off-season : winter (exclusive of professional shows) and August* ♦ *Credit cards : American Express, Diners and Visa* ♦ *Facilities : reservations, laundry, dry-cleaning* ♦ *Dogs allowed* ♦ *Parking facilities : opposite 169 boulevard Saint-Germain and place Saint-Sulpice* ♦ *Transportation : Metro station Saint-Germain-des-Prés - Buses 39, 48, 58, 63, 70, 84, 86, 87, 95 and 96.*

The Saint-Germain-des-Prés church tower and the statue of Diderot watch over this hotel with balconies, a pretty awning and heavy white curtains, a bit set back from the boulevard…
Inside, two things catch the eye : an imposing marble basin hiding under greenery, and beneath the lobby, the large oval shape, lit by a glass roof, and extending toward the painting in trompe-l'œil of a handrail, then opening onto an exotic landscape… The rest is classic. Careful comfort in the rooms where pastel shades and soft prints are in harmony with pretty copies. 19th century squat armchairs, chest of drawers and tables ; lights, cupboards or wardrobes, everything is well designed. Beautiful Italian style bathrooms, where the faience tiles draw large rugs on the floor. We like best the rooms on the street side where you have view on the church (and from the upper floors on Saint-Eustache, Beaubourg and the Sacré-Cœur). But those overlooking the courtyard are nicer in the summer… despite the receptionists, always in a hurry, you'll find people here helpful : a tiny car is to the clintele's disposal !

Hôtel du Pas-de-Calais ★★★

59 rue des Saints-Pères - 75006 Paris
Tel. : (1) 45 48 78 74 - Telex : 270 476 - Fax : (1) 45 44 94 57
Manager : Mr Teissèdre

♦ *41 rooms, sound-proofed on the street side, with bath (1 with shower), direct dial line, TV by satellite, hair-drier and safe* ♦ *Patio* ♦ *Prices : single : 560 F ; double : 690 F - Extra bed : 140 F* ♦ *Breakfast included* ♦ *Off-season : 15 December to February and August* ♦ *Credit cards : Eurocard, MasterCard and Visa* ♦ *Facilities : reservations, laundry, dry-cleaning* ♦ *Dogs allowed* ♦ *Parking facilities : opposite 169 boulevard Saint-Germain* ♦ *Transportation : Metro station Saint-Germain-des-Prés, RER Gare d'Orsay - Buses 39, 48, 63, 68, 70, 84, 86, 87, 94, 95 and 96.*

In this district where hotels are so numerous, this one is different because of its decoration carefully looked after over the past twenty years. Apart from the modern lobby with smooth materials and sandy shades, the rest of the hotel is decorated in the style of the 1970s. If you like kitsch, ask for room #63 : chocolate-coloured satinwood and a dropped bed frame, the walls are striped brown and beige, the curtains and bedspread are in a reddish brown print fabric with big round trees. Ten years ago, such a decoration would have put you off but nowadays, it is surprising and tomorrow it may be listed as an ancient monument ! Except if it disappears while the rooms are under renovation. In the attic there is one large room furnished in country style with beams and white woolen curtains, a reference to old converted attics. The rooms on the mezzanine floor are low-ceilinged and dark, but those giving on the courtyard are light at noon ; the ones on the ground floor giving on the garden are very agreeable. Notice the elegant bathtubs of enamelled sandstone. And here is a detail of importance : the manager was born in this house.

Hôtel des Saints-Pères ★★★

65 rue des Saints-Pères - 75006 Paris
Tel. : (1) 45 44 50 00 - Telex : 205 424 - Fax : (1) 45 44 90 83
Manager : Mr Lingrand

♦ *37 sound-proofed rooms and suites with shower or bath, direct dial line, TV, safe and minibar* ♦ *Patio, bar* ♦ *Prices : single or double : 400 to 1 000 F ; suite : 1 250 to 1 500 F* ♦ *Breakfast : 45 F* ♦ *Off-season : August* ♦ *Credit cards : Eurocard, MasterCard and Visa* ♦ *Facilities : reservations, laundry, dry-cleaning, snacks* ♦ *No dogs allowed* ♦ *Parking facilities : opposite 169 boulevard Saint-Germain* ♦ *Transportation : Metro station Saint-Germain-des-Prés - Buses 39, 48, 63, 70, 84, 86, 87 and 95.*

The interior decoration of this hotel is light, almost transparent. It is organized around an exquisite patio surmounted by the building's 17th century fronton, on one of the walls hangs a funny black wall clock. The patio on which open most of the rooms, is right next to a sitting room, a bar and a dining room with lovely pink tablecloths. Mr Lingrand has conceived very cosy rooms : silent, quite large, carefully furnished, with really large wardrobes and adjoining refined bathrooms. The furniture is a combination of bamboo and beautiful chintz which imparts a simple charm to the rooms. The unique and sublime room called "the fresco" (a magnificent allegory is painted on the ceiling) displays 18th century splendours in deep blue shades. The bathroom is faithful to this style and only a screen keeps it out of sight. The welcome is elegant but slightly distant, however, this hotel is almost perfect and well implanted in the district.

Hôtel Lenox - Saint-Germain ★★★

9 rue de l'Université - 75007 Paris
Tel. : (1) 42 96 10 95 - Telex : 260 745 - Fax : (1) 42 61 52 83
Manager : Mr de Contenson

♦ *34 rooms (5 with mezzanine) with shower or bath, direct dial line and* TV ♦ *Bar* ♦ *Prices : single : 470 F ; double : 480 to 620 F ; suite : 790 F* ♦ *Breakfast : 40 F* ♦ *Off-season : January and August* ♦ *Credit cards : American Express, Diners, Eurocard, MasterCard and Visa* ♦ *Facilities : reservations, laundry, dry-cleaning, snacks* ♦ *No dogs allowed* ♦ *Parking facilities : 9 rue de Montalembert and opposite 169 boulevard Saint-Germain* ♦ *Transportation : Metro stations Rue-du-Bac or Saint-Germain-des-Prés, RER Gare d'Orsay - Buses 24, 27, 39, 48, 63, 68, 69, 70, 87 and 95.*

At the corner where meet the pretty rues du Pré-aux-Clercs and de l'Université, the Lenox has managed to attract a young, up-to-date and elegant clientele, faithful to the 1930 sharp lines of the bar, open until 1 am. Through large French windows with a brass knob, you enter the classic and refined universe of this hotel. Faded shades, beige for the walls and the columns at the entrance, grey for the sofas, brown and beige marble flooring with an oriental rug and chintz curtains to add a touch of warmth. In the same way, a combination of old and modern furnishing give character to the rooms hung with large mirrors and where lighting is well distributed. The white bathrooms are enhanced by a green or blue mosaic edge. Beautiful and cheerful. The beams, when there is any, are painted white in order to alleviate the proportions of the too small rooms, the corner rooms have a mezzanine and two windows, they open on the balcony running along the fourth floor, those on the fifth floor have sloping ceilings and small private balconies. Too bad for the other rooms...

Hôtel de l'Université ★★★

22 rue de l'Université - 75007 Paris
Tel. : (1) 42 61 09 39 - Telex : 260 717 - Fax : (1) 42 60 40 84
Manager : Mrs Bergmann

♦ *28 rooms with shower or bath, direct dial line, TV and safe*
♦ *Bar* ♦ *Prices : single with shower (no WC) : 400 F, with shower : 500 F, with bath : 550 F ; double : 550 to 1 200 F - Extra bed : 30%* ♦ *Continental breakfast : 20 F ; with orange juice and cheese : 45 F* ♦ *Off-season : August* ♦ *No credit cards accepted*
♦ *Facilities : reservations, laundry, dry-cleaning, snacks* ♦ *No dogs allowed* ♦ *Parking facilities : 9 rue de Montalembert and opposite 169 boulevard Saint-Germain* ♦ *Transportation : Metro stations Rue-du-Bac or Saint-Germain-des-Prés, RER Gare d'Orsay - Invalides air terminal- Buses 24, 27, 39, 48, 63, 68, 69, 70, 87 and 95.*

This used to be a town house and all its dimensions were used to advantage (the vault shelters the entrance hall, a lobby and small sitting rooms), the entrance is decorated with a discreet distinction. The stairs and the sustaining wooden pillars were kept. A light well brightens the sandstone flooring. Nowhere can you see pretention, only fine taste : the armchairs are in turnery wood, the sofas have velvet cushions and the lounge is a bit lower than the small dining room where breakfast and snacks are served. On the stone walls, sometimes masked under stud work, hang pictures of landscapes, a beautiful brass chandelier and wooden bracket lamps. The rooms are all different, they sometimes have a fireplace and always old weathered and comfortable furniture : a couch, tub chairs, a chest of drawers and little round table. All those pieces bear the charm of objects bought one by one, for the pleasure of the inhabitants. For more luminosity, the moquette is of a soft yellow colour and the walls are covered with Japanese wallpapers or damask cotton fabric. This is better than a hotel, it is a friends' house.

Hôtel Montalembert ★★★★

3 rue de Montalembert - 75007 Paris
Tel. : (1) 45 48 68 11 - Telex : 200 132 - Fax : (1) 42 22 58 19
Manager : Mr Desnos

♦ *51 rooms and 5 suites, sound-proofed and air-conditioned, with bath, direct dial line, TV and video (all systems), hair-drier, safe and minibar* ♦ *American bar, restaurant, conference room* ♦ *Prices : single : 1 350 F ; double : 1 550 to 1 700 F ; suite : 2 200 to 2 800 F - Extra bed : 300 F* ♦ *Breakfast : 80 F* ♦ *Off-season : December and January (exclusive of professional shows) and August* ♦ *Credit cards : American Express, Diners and Visa* ♦ *Facilities : all those of its category, snacks* ♦ *No dogs allowed* ♦ *Parking facilities : Montalembert car park* ♦ *Transportation : Metro station Rue-du-Bac, RER Gare d'Orsay - Buses 24, 63, 68, 69, 83, 84 and 94.*

The Faubourg Saint-Germain finally has a hotel which really fits in : the Montalembert. Built in 1926, this hotel which used to be slightly old-fashioned has come out of its shell this summer, adorned with the graces imparted to the alliance both of luxury and mesure. Graphic, almost nude in the black and white space of the entrance, the hotel created, around a fireplace, a delicious living room where you won't feel the time passing by : honey-coloured armchairs on which red cushions flame, golden light, canopy filtering the light coming from the mini-patio, small tables made for a glass or a book – borrowed from the library (a real one, for informed readers). Same success for the rooms and suites, contemporary with rosewood furniture, or Louis-Philippe style. All have flawless comfort and lights, impeccable black and white-striped duvets, refined bathrooms covered with grey marble. A new great address for a discreetly fashionable clientele.

Hôtel Verneuil-Saint-Germain ★★★

8 rue de Verneuil - 75007 Paris
Tel. : (1) 42 60 82 14 / 42 60 24 16 - Telex : 211 608
Fax : (1) 42 61 40 38 - Manager : Mrs Chekroun

♦ *26 rooms with bath, direct dial line, TV, hair-drier* ♦ *Bar*
♦ *Prices : single : 610 F ; double : 640 F - Extra bed : 175 F*
♦ *Breakfast with orange juice : 35 F* ♦ *Off-season : November and December (exclusive of professional shows) and August*
♦ *Credit cards : American Express, Diners and Visa* ♦ *Facilities : reservations, laundry, dry-cleaning, snacks, secretarial work*
♦ *Dogs allowed* ♦ *Parking facilities : 9 rue de Montalembert*
♦ *Transportation : Metro stations Rue-du-Bac or Saint-Germain-des-Prés, RER Gare d'Orsay - Invalides air terminal - Buses 24, 27, 39, 48, 63, 68, 69, 86, 87, 95 and 96.*

In one of Paris most beautiful streets, the oval sign and the lanterns at the entrance, surrounded by four evergreens are so attractive that you are drawn to go inside. It is obvious that to decorate the hotel in this classic but still unexpected style gave great pleasure. In the lobby, a mirror wall, the other walls are bright blue pigmented with white and softened by dark multicoloured striped curtains. The cosy lounge-bar is furnished in Régence style and decorated with a Medieval mirror and big bouquets of flowers. The rooms are furnished in Directoire style, they are pink or blue with flowered fabrics and embroidered tablecloths. In the bathrooms are marble framed mirrors. Surrounded by gardens, the hotel benefits from a view onto trees from the upper floors on the back side and onto zinc roofs on the street side. Conferences can be held in the vaulted cellars embelished by a stone basin. When we came the lift still held the fragance of heath and evergreen branches brought upstairs to decorate the balconies. Here, the air you breath is festive and envigorating.

Hôtel Bersoly's ★★★

28 rue de Lille - 75007 Paris
Tel. : (1) 42 60 73 79 - Telex : 217 505 - Fax : (1) 49 27 05 55
Manager : Mrs Carbonnaux

♦ *Closed from 15 to 31 August* ♦ *16 sound-proofed rooms (air-conditioned on the 5th floor), with shower or bath, direct dial line, TV, hair-drier and safe* ♦ *Bar* ♦ *Prices : single or double : 500 to 580 F - Extra bed : 100 F* ♦ *Breakfast with fruit juice : 40 F* ♦ *Off-season : December to February* ♦ *Credit cards : Eurocard, MasterCard and Visa* ♦ *Facilities : reservations, laundry, dry-cleaning, snacks* ♦ *Dogs allowed* ♦ *Parking facilities : 9 rue de Montalembert and opposite 169 boulevard Saint-Germain* ♦ *Transportation : Metro stations Rue-du-Bac and Solférino, RER Gare d'Orsay - Invalides air terminal - Buses 24, 27, 39, 48, 63, 68, 69, 86, 87 and 95.*

This is again an old house arranged with taste and simplicity, where you will be warmly welcomed. Among the details pertaining to this place are the ancient stone flooring, carefully preserved, and the fine and light handrail of wrought iron. The atmosphere is cosy. You also feel at home in the rooms, even though they are not very large, except those on the fifth floor. The decoration is country Louis XV style for the cupboards and the weathered writing desks, 19th century for the chairs and armchairs. The herring-bone patterned material is in a harmony of pink or yellow (pervading the floor of the small, white bathrooms). They look like guest rooms, named Chagall, Chardin, Picasso, Renoir or Douanier-Rousseau... depending on the lithography pinned to the wall. Remember the large rooms on the fifth floor (one of the bathrooms is on two levels), and those on the ground floor, benefiting from the tiny patio. The breakfast room and the lounge were arranged in the basement.

Hôtel de Lille ★★

40 rue de Lille - 75007 Paris
Tel. : (1) 42 61 29 09 - Telex : 240 510
Manager : Mr Margouilla

♦ *Closed from 28 July to 19 August and Christmas* ♦ *20 sound-proofed rooms with shower or bath, direct dial line, TV* ♦ *Prices : single or double : 450 to 600 F* ♦ *Breakfast with orange juice : 30 F* ♦ *No off-season* ♦ *Credit cards : American Express, Diners and Visa* ♦ *Facilities : reservations, laundry, dry-cleaning* ♦ *No dogs allowed* ♦ *Parking facilities : 9 rue de Montalembert and opposite 169 boulevard Saint-Germain* ♦ *Transportation : Metro stations Rue-du-Bac or Saint-Germain-des-Prés, RER Gare d'Orsay - Invalides air terminal - Buses 24, 27, 39, 48, 63, 68, 69, 86, 87 and 95.*

A wonderful location for this tiny hotel which has managed to take advantage of it : the Seine river, the Tuileries Gardens, the Louvre and Orsay museums are within a stone's throw and Saint-Germain-des-Prés five minutes away.

The management made the best out of the house's small proportions, creating a smooth lobby where a black desk and comfortable green armchairs contrast with the beige walls and the floor's large and shiny tiles. In the back, a bar, not large but welcoming. The surprise is a living room in the basement, well lit and very comfortable, under arches opening out from a gigantic centered pilar... The rooms are minute, but airy thanks to the well adapted furniture (clever chest of drawers-davenport) of burr elm or ginger-coloured bamboo which add some colour to the beige roughcast. The showers dominate in the bathrooms which are impeccably covered in blue or beige faience. A very refined hotel for its 2 stars, in one of Paris nicest areas : what a privilege !

Hôtel du Quai Voltaire ★★

19 quai Voltaire - 75007 Paris
Tel. : (1) 42 61 50 91 - Fax : (1) 42 61 62 26
Manager : Mr Etchenique

♦ *33 rooms with shower or bath, direct dial line, TV upon request*
♦ *Bar* ♦ *Prices : single with shower : 390 F, with bath : 440 to 475 F ; double with bath : 530 to 590 F ; triple : 700 F - Extra bed : 100 F* ♦ *Breakfast : 35 F* ♦ *Off-season : January and February* ♦ *Credit cards : American Express, Diners and Visa* ♦ *Facilities : reservations, laundry, dry-cleaning, snacks* ♦ *No dogs allowed* ♦ *Parking facilities : 9 rue de Montalembert* ♦ *Transportation : Metro station Rue-du-Bac, RER Gare d'Orsay - Invalides air terminal - Buses 24, 27, 39, 48, 63, 68, 69 and 95.*

This hotel was meant for people who love the Seine river, located in the antique dealers' district, it faces the Louvre and is near the Orsay museum. Here stayed Nimier and Baudelaire, Oscar Wilde, Sibelius, Wagner and Pissarro who painted "Le Pont Royal" looking out of the window of his room. Too bad the lobby lacks charater (but the welcome is first class), it contrasts with the sitting room and the bar. In the lounge, a blue and yellow Medieval tapestry, 19th century furniture, woodworks and a big centre light of the 1950s. The bar, where breakfast is served, is even more 1950, with moleskin chairs and benches, the map of Paris pinned to the wall. All is comfortable... and nowadays, avant-garde. The rooms are well proportioned but they have no double windows to protect you from the street noise. Therefore, ask for one of the six back rooms. Everywhere the taste is simple and discerning : wallpaper showing small flowers, brass beds, Louis XVI or 19th century furniture, paintings of Paris as seen from the hotel. The bathrooms made in the 1960s are old-fashioned but very clean and large (especially in the back rooms).

Hôtel Duc de Saint-Simon ★★★

14 rue de Saint-Simon - 75007 Paris
Tel. : (1) 45 48 35 66 - Telex : 203 277 - Fax : (1) 45 48 68 25
Manager : Mr Lindqvist

◆ *34 air-conditioned rooms and suites with bath (1 with shower), direct dial line, TV upon request, hair-drier* ◆ *Private terraces, bar* ◆ *Prices : single or double : 900 to 1 350 F ; suite : 1 450 to 1 800 F - Extra bed : + 30%* ◆ *Breakfast : 70 F* ◆ *Off-season : August* ◆ *No credit cards accepted* ◆ *Facilities : reservations, laundry, dry-cleaning, snacks* ◆ *No dogs allowed* ◆ *Parking facilities : 30 boulevard Raspail* ◆ *Transportation : Metro station Rue-du-Bac, RER Gare d'Orsay - Buses 63, 68, 69, 83, 84 and 94.*

In this district where every town house hides a secret garden behind its high walls, the gates of this hotel widely open, show a scenery : a square, paved courtyard flowered with nasturtium and laurel, lighted in the evening through the French windows of a white house built at the beginning of the 19th century. Above, there is a terrace overwhelmed by green plants where a few of the rooms open... The back of the house looks out onto the trees planted in the surrounding private gardens. Inside, the decoration is very pleasing : extremely refined, subtle colours and lights. The rooms are comfortable and quiet, most of them give on a garden and four of them have a terrace.

A strange trompe-l'œil covers the walls of the vestibule, stairway and even the lift (gnarled elm wood and imitation marble). In the rooms, sometimes small, the decoration is Anglo-French. An ultimate refinement : monogrammed sheets and towels, silverware and toast for breakfast. One of Paris highly esteemed hotel of character meant for a clientele who can afford it.

Hôtel de Nevers ★★

83 rue du Bac - 75007 Paris
Tel. : (1) 45 44 61 30
Manager : Mrs Ireland

♦ *11 rooms with shower or bath, direct dial line and minibar* ♦ *No lift* ♦ *Prices : single : 295 F ; double : 345 F to 360 F - Extra bed : 70 F* ♦ *Breakfast with fruit juice and yogurt : 25 F* ♦ *Off-season : winter (exclusive of professional shows)* ♦ *No credit cards accepted* ♦ *Facilities : reservations, laundry, dry-cleaning, snacks* ♦ *Dogs allowed* ♦ *Parking facilities : 30 boulevard Raspail* ♦ *Transportation : Metro station Rue-du-Bac - Buses 63, 68, 69, 83, 84 and 94.*

Don't miss it ! The building is so modest that it could go unseen if the façade of the neighbouring house did not draw your attention. A former dependence of the Récollettes convent, this tiny little house still has a wicket gate and a curious mantelpiece in the flowered entrance brightened by a large mirror. A stairway with white steps goes up to the rooms ; it is easy to climb because the eye is caught by a large still life painting and 19th century engravings hung alongway. The rooms are all different, luminous and soft, they rarely are on the landing's level : the manager played with the existing levels and volumes to keep a "nunnery-like" atmosphere. The rooms on the top floor have sloping ceilings, a step goes down to the bathroom and the windows open onto terraces arranged on the roof. Rustic furnishing, caramel-coloured curtains, flowered bedspreads match the pale-pink wallcovering. On each floor you'll find a lounge-dining room corner next to a doll-like kitchen out of which the smell of coffee and toast says much about the quality of the welcome : simply charming. Here, people rarely say no.

Hôtel de Suède ★★★

31 rue Vaneau - 75007 Paris
Tel. : (1) 47 05 00 08 - Telex : 200 596 - Fax : (1) 47 05 69 27
Manager : Mr Chesnot

♦ *41 rooms with washbasins, shower or bath, direct dial line (5 with TV)* ♦ *Prices : single : 505 F ; double : 555 F ; triple : 755 F ; suite : 980 F* ♦ *Breakfast included* ♦ *Off-season : winter (exclusive of professional shows)* ♦ *Credit cards : American Express, Eurocard, MasterCard and Visa* ♦ *Facilities : reservations, laundry, dry-cleaning, snacks* ♦ *No dogs allowed* ♦ *Parking facilities : 30 boulevard Raspail and square Boucicaut* ♦ *Transportation : Metro stations Saint-François-Xavier or Sèvres-Babylone - Invalides air terminal - Buses 82, 87 and 92.*

This is a pretty building with white shutters, it stands in a silent street near ministries and embassies. Inside, through a lobby decorated in Directoire style you can look at the gardens of the Hôtel Matignon (residence of the Prime Minister). Everything is in grey nuances apart from the woodwork in the sitting room. But what is most attractive in this hotel is the view on the courtyard (fine sandy gravel bordered with balsamine) and the wide view on the Matignon trees from the third floor rooms ; these are brighter and more cheerful (although smaller) than the front rooms where grey is not enhanced by daylight. All have some things in common : an inkstand with a leather flap and a modern, impeccable bathroom with grey tiling of course. Notice the apartment in the pavilion, it is vast and well furnished with a round table in cherry wood and decorated with engravings showing the Chantilly and Marly Châteaux.

Hôtel de Bourgogne and Montana ★★★

3 rue de Bourgogne - 75007 Paris
Tel. : (1) 45 51 20 22 - Telex : 270 854 - Fax : (1) 45 56 11 98
Manager : Mrs Dupont

♦ *30 rooms and 5 suites, sound-proofed, with shower or bath, direct dial line and TV* ♦ *Restaurant (closed in August and on weekends), bar, conference room* ♦ *Prices : single : 500 to 683 F ; double : 720 to 750 F ; suite : 950 F - Extra bed : 300 F* ♦ *Breakfast with orange juice : included* ♦ *Off-season : December, January and August* ♦ *Credit cards : American Express, Diners, Eurocard, MasterCard and Visa* ♦ *Facilities : reservations, snacks* ♦ *Dogs allowed* ♦ *Parking facilities : Esplanade des Invalides* ♦ *Transportation : Metro stations Assemblée-Nationale or Invalides, RER Gare d'Orsay - Invalides air terminal - Buses 24, 63, 69, 73, 83, 84, 93 and 94.*

Near the place du Palais Bourbon, this hotel owes its quality to its location. And to a superb rotunda with pink marble columns and large mirrors surmounted by an octogonal gallery. This used to be the hallway of an old town house. The bar has just now been panelled in mahogany ; the old rounded lift closed by a gate still goes upstairs. The first floor is actually a mezzanine floor and here although they are low-ceilinged the rooms are well proportioned and have charming half-moon windows. We recommend the back rooms because the rue de Bourgogne is a busy street ; particularly nice are those on the top floors with a view over the Palais Bourbon and the Concorde, or the small rooms on the sixth floor overlooking the trees of the Ministry of Defense. The welcome is pleasant and professional : this hotel has been a family business since 1929.

Hôtel de Varenne ★★★

44 rue de Bourgogne - 75007 Paris
Tel. : (1) 45 51 45 55 - Telex : 205 329 - Fax : (1) 45 51 86 63
Manager : Mrs Cherruy

♦ 24 sound-proofed rooms with shower or bath, direct dial line and TV ♦ Flowered courtyard ♦ Prices : double : 430 to 580 F ; triple : 600 F - Extra bed : 100 F ♦ Breakfast : 35 F ♦ Off-season : August ♦ Credit cards : American Express, Eurocard and Visa ♦ Facilities : reservations, laundry, dry-cleaning ♦ Dogs allowed ♦ Parking facilities : Esplanade des Invalides ♦ Transportation : Metro station Chambre-des-Députés, RER Invalides - Invalides air terminal - Buses 63, 69, 83, 84 and 94.

The façade giving on the rue de Bourgogne is not all there is to it, actually, most of the hotel building stretches along a quite large interior courtyard where green plants are so abundant that on sunny days you can have a drink or breakfast outside (most of the rooms do not give on the noisy rue de Bourgogne). Two lanterns light the front door opening onto beige and black flooring. The cane English furniture is nice, the brown moquette and wallpaper are enhanced by the white ceilings and the small paned, wooden framed large windows. In the rooms, brown was eliminated and replaced by pastel colours, as for the rest, chintz curtains and bedspreads, lead-white wooden furniture. Now that they are renovated, their nice proportions show and although they are low-ceilinged, they are quite light from the second floor up.

Hôtel Elysées-Maubourg ★★★

35 boulevard de Latour-Maubourg - 75007 Paris
Tel. : (1) 45 56 10 78 - Telex : 206 227 - Fax : (1) 47 05 65 08
Manager : Melle Guérin

♦ *30 rooms with bath, direct dial line, TV (Canal+ and video), hair-drier and safe* ♦ *Bar, sauna, patio* ♦ *Prices : single : 510 F ; double : 640 to 690 F ; suite : 720 F - Extra bed : + 20%* ♦ *Breakfast with orange juice : included* ♦ *Off-season : December, January and August* ♦ *Credit cards : American Express, Diners, En Route, Eurocard, MasterCard and Visa* ♦ *Facilities : reservations, laundry, dry-cleaning* ♦ *Dogs allowed* ♦ *Parking facilities : Esplanade des Invalides* ♦ *Transportation : Metro station Latour-Maubourg, RER Pont-de-l'Alma - Invalides air terminal - Buses 28, 49, 63, 69 and 83.*

This hotel is a model for comfort, it is located on an avenue planted with plane trees, very silent in the evening and is near the Champs-Elysées but on the left bank of the Seine river.

The lobby is very modern, decorated with good quality materials : marble, gnarled elm wood, black leather and large windows overlooking a patio with green trellis which are covered by climbing plants in the summer and where you can eat breakfast or have a drink.

The major asset of the rooms is their size but obviously the larger ones were reserved to twin beds. The decoration is classic, beige, soft green or blue ; plain curtains matching modern bathrooms ; bamboo furniture, Louis-Philippe style or else and nicest of all cane Louis XVI ; reproductions of landscapes hang on the walls and in the four top floor rooms, there are large luminous picture windows.

Les Jardins d'Eiffel ★★★

8 rue Amélie - 75007 Paris
Tel. : (1) 47 05 46 21 - Telex : 206 582 - Fax : (1) 45 55 28 08
Manager : Mr Rech

♦ *44 rooms, sound-proofed on the street side, with bath, direct dial line, TV by satellite and Canal+, hair-drier, trouser-press, safe and minibar* ♦ *Patio-courtyard, sauna, conference room* ♦ *Prices : single : 620 F ; double : 690 F ; triple with bath : 800 F ; suite : 1 350 F* ♦ *Breakfast with orange juice, eggs and cheese : 35 F* ♦ *Off-season : 15 December to 1 March, July and August* ♦ *Credit cards : American Express, Diners and Visa* ♦ *Facilities : reservations, laundry, dry-cleaning, snacks* ♦ *Dogs allowed* ♦ *Parking facilities : 15 spaces in the hotel* ♦ *Transportation : Metro station Latour-Maubourg, RER Pont-de-l'Alma or Invalides - Invalides air terminal - Buses 28, 49, 69, 80 and 92.*

This insignificant street linking the rue Saint-Dominique to the rue de Grenelle shelters a well arranged and managed hotel. The lobby is furnished in Louis XVI style, further on are a lounge and an elegant breakfast room giving on a winter garden. Large grey leather sofas match the predominant pink. The rooms are not large, but one feels comfortable in them, especially on the third floor and above, on the courtyard side, from which you dominate the opposite buildings : from the third floor the Eiffel Tower shows its peak and appears completely from the fourth and fifth floors. We prefer the back rooms, more luminous in the afternoon or the front rooms whose number ends with 4, larger with two windows. Some of them communicate and can be turned into apartments. As for bathrooms, they are in marble, small and well equipped. The careful welcome, service and comfort, the possibility to transform the dining room into a conference room make this hotel a priviledged place for businessmen too.

Hôtel de la Tulipe ★★

33 rue Malar - 75007 Paris
Tel. : (1) 45 51 67 21 - Telex : 264 918
Manager : Mr Fortuit

♦ *20 rooms, sound-proofed on the street side, with shower or bath, direct dial line, TV and minibar* ♦ *Patio* ♦ *Prices : single : 358 F ; double : 408 to 488 F ; triple : 465 to 555 F* ♦ *Breakfast with cheese : 30 F* ♦ *Off-season : December and January* ♦ *Credit cards : American Express, Eurocard, MasterCard and Visa* ♦ *Facilities : reservations, laundry, dry-cleaning* ♦ *Dogs allowed* ♦ *Parking facilities : Esplanade des Invalides* ♦ *Transportation : Metro stations Latour-Maubourg or Invalides, RER Pont-de-l'Alma - Invalides air terminal - Buses 28, 49, 63, 69, 80, 83 and 92.*

In a residential area, very appreciated because it is near the business centres but quiet in the evening, this little hotel used to be a convent. The walls of the cells were pulled down to make the twenty rooms slightly bigger. Some are arranged around a paved courtyard where balsamine and geranium bloom in season and which is permanently covered with superb ivy. About ten rooms give on this garden, the front rooms have double windows (useless when night comes). You rapidly feel at home in the sitting room-lobby : low, comfortable, white leather armchairs go well with the flooring, the beams and the Louis XIII chairs. Big bouquets of dried flowers stand in pewter pots. The adjoining breakfast room is just as nice. In the rooms, priority was given to the practical side : claret-coloured moquette, pink or beige Japanese wallpaper, tint bamboo and stone walls. This is a bit heavy, but here also, you feel comfortable (the large grey or garnet red bathroom tiles have more character). A nice place to stay, thanks to the staff's simplicity.

Hôtel Saint-Dominique ★★

62 rue Saint-Dominique - 75007 Paris
Tel. : (1) 47 05 51 44 - Telex : 206 968 - Fax : (1) 47 05 81 28
Managers : Mrs Petit and Mr Tible

♦ *34 rooms with shower or bath, direct dial line, TV, hair-drier, safe and minibar* ♦ *Prices : single : 420 F ; double : 450 and 460 F ; triple : 580 to 630 F - Extra bed : 80 F* ♦ *Breakfast with orange juice and cheese : 38 F* ♦ *Off-season : February and August* ♦ *Credit cards : American Express, Diners, Eurocard, MasterCard and Visa* ♦ *Facilities : reservations, laundry, dry-cleaning* ♦ *Dogs allowed* ♦ *Parking facilities : Esplanade des Invalides* ♦ *Transportation : Metro stations Latour-Maubourg or Invalides, RER Pont-de-l'Alma - Invalides air terminal - Buses 28, 42, 49, 69, 80 and 92.*

This is an English cottage in the middle of the 7th arrondissement, and, like the two other members of the small group Centre-Ville, is a complete success. Well located, and skillfully renovated the Saint-Dominique has a lot of character : a large bay window with small panes, pine wood furnishing, Club armchairs for the sitting room corner, two beautiful gilt mirrors to enhance the beige walls and moquette. Two thirds of the rooms give on two small, paved courtyards, flowered in summer. The windows are green and this is enough to make you feel as if you were in the South of France. All the rooms are charming. They are decorated now with a wallpaper showing wild flowers and embroidered cotton curtains, now with Provençal patterns which also show on the bathroom floor, the rest of it is white. Some of the beds have brass frames, the pine wood furnishing is light-coloured, practical and pretty. In the larger rooms you'll find comfortable armchairs, a chest of drawers or a small sofa. These pieces add to the comfort, be it of English or Provençal inspiration, this doesn't matter.

Hôtel Lecourbe ★★

28 rue Lecourbe - 75015 Paris
Tel. : (1) 47 34 49 06 - Telex : 205 440 - Fax : (1) 47 34 64 65
Manager : Mr Andregnette

♦ *43 rooms and 4 suites with shower or bath, direct dial line, TV, hair-drier, safe and minibar* ♦ *Patio, conference room* ♦ *Prices : single : 350 F ; double : 400 F ; suite : 540 F* ♦ *Breakfast : 30 F* ♦ *Off-season : winter (exclusive of professional shows)* ♦ *Credit cards : American Express, Diners and Visa* ♦ *Facilities : reservations, laundry, dry-cleaning, snacks* ♦ *Dogs allowed* ♦ *Parking facilities : 28 rue François-Bonvin* ♦ *Transportation : Metro stations Sèvres-Lecourbe or Volontaires - Buses 28, 39, 70 and 89.*

On the border between the 15th and the 7th arrondissements, in a residential area, a raised façade of beige bricks hides one of Paris most charming hotels. Forming a quadrilateral around a garden, it looks in every respect like an old (renovated !) district convent. Most of the rooms give on this patio where honeysuckle, roses and perennial bushes grow freely. The rooms are pale blue or salmon pink, furnished in a rustic style, and the bathrooms are well equipped. The palm goes to the rooms with sloping ceilings and to the singles overlooking the garden. The breakfast room is decorated in country style in agreement with the menu : fruit juices, cheese, rillettes, corn flakes and compote ! The conference room, arranged in a professional way is the last touch to this delightful hotel.

Hôtel Montcalm ★★★

50 avenue Félix-Faure - 75015 Paris
Tel. : (1) 45 54 97 27 - Telex : 203 174 - Fax : (1) 45 54 15 05
Manager : Mrs Brochoire

♦ *41 rooms with bath, direct dial line, TV and minibar* ♦ *Tiny garden* ♦ *Prices : single : 450 and 470 F ; double : 500 and 530 F ; triple : 635 and 665 F - Extra bed : 160 F* ♦ *Breakfast : 25 F* ♦ *Off-season : July and August* ♦ *Credit cards : American Express, Diners and Visa* ♦ *Facilities : reservations, laundry, dry-cleaning* ♦ *No dogs allowed* ♦ *Parking facilities : 94 rue de la Convention* ♦ *Transportation : Metro station Boucicaut, RER Javel or Champ-de-Mars - Buses 42, 62 and 70.*

Many comfortable but uninteresting hotels opened lately in this arrondissement near the Parc des Exposition and the Porte de Versailles. Here, in the courtyard, flowered lawns are as small as stamps, they draw careful curves between which several tables can stand. This hotel seems to be an exception and a good surprise on this wide avenue bordered with trees and in an area both shopping and residential where dull hotels abound. The lobby leads to a small and amusing veranda jutting out over the courtyard. Long and comfortable couches of honey-coloured leather and plaited straw furniture for the sitting room. The rooms are unpretentious but the details express an undefinable charm : in the old beige and brown rooms, an off-white bedspread showing small geometrical patterns matches the curtains ; in the renovated ones – nuances of faded pink and sea green. Although the quite large rooms with twin beds shall often be offered to one person, there are also some small, pretty singles organized with the same comfort and giving on the garden.

Hôtel Wallace ★★★

89 rue Fondary - 75015 Paris
Tel. : (1) 45 78 83 30 - Telex : 205 277 - Fax : (1) 40 58 19 43
Manager : Mr Lachampt

♦ *35 rooms with bath, TV and minibar, direct dial line* ♦ *Patio* ♦ *Prices : single : 450 F ; double : 450 to 490 F - Extra bed : 100 F* ♦ *Breakfast with fruit juice and cheese : 35 F* ♦ *Off-season : 1 November to 15 March, July and August* ♦ *Credit cards : American Express, Diners, Eurocard, JCB, MasterCard and Visa* ♦ *Facilities : reservations, laundry, dry-cleaning* ♦ *Dogs allowed* ♦ *Parking facilities : rue Cambronne* ♦ *Transportation : Metro station Emile-Zola - Buses 49, 70 and 80.*

Light-coloured roughcast, pink tiled roof, two floors on the street side : an air of country inn in the centre of Paris. The tiny garden is surrounded by an entirely white building around which big brown wooden galleries run, you can catch a glimpse of them through the glass doors…

But it is also a hotel completely and tastefully renovated. The surrounding glass doors light up the beige lobby, beige pervades everything here : black-veined marble flooring in the entrance and lobby ; lit up by big soft-coloured bunches of flowers on the cotton fabric covering the armchairs and sofas in the living room, as well as on the chintz of the bedspreads ; plain (but shaded with pink or blue depending on the rooms) as wallcoverings, likewise for the light wood armchairs in the rooms, which stand out on the plum-coloured moquette… Impeccable, well designed, with clean bathrooms, these rooms are charming, even the smaller ones and those in the attic. Most of them overlook the garden where plantations seem promising (bushes, geraniums, ivy) : another year or two and it will look gorgeous. And to think that we are but a few minutes away from the Porte de Versailles !

Hôtel Frémiet ★★★

6 avenue Frémiet - 75016 Paris
Tel. : (1) 45 24 52 06 - Telex : 630 329 - Fax : (1) 42 88 77 46
Managers : Mr and Mrs Fourmond

♦ *34 rooms and 2 suites, sound-proofed and air-conditioned, with shower or bath, direct dial line, TV, hair-drier and minibar* ♦ *Prices : single : 515 to 680 F ; double : 725 to 795 F ; suite : 885 to 1 280F - Extra bed : 150 F* ♦ *Breakfast included* ♦ *Off-season : winter (exclusive of professional shows) and August* ♦ *Credit cards : American Express, Diners and Visa* ♦ *Facilities : reservations, laundry, dry-cleaning, snacks* ♦ *Dogs allowed* ♦ *Parking facilities : avenue Frémiet (no parking meters) and 12 avenue Marcel-Proust* ♦ *Transportation : Metro station Passy, RER Champ-de-Mars - Buses 32, 70 and 72.*

This is a particularly well hidden hotel, it stands almost on the embankment, but at the foot of the hill of Passy, in the passageway leading to the cellars of the Wine museum, which are almost directly underneath Balzac's house. If there is one place isolated from the bustling city, this is it, even though the elevated metro is nearby and Radio-France House, some hundred yards away. Nothing extraordinary on sight in this traditional hotel decorated in 1970s style. However, the scarecity of hotels in this area, the extreme care with which it was sound-proofed, its comfort, the nice size of all the rooms decorated in a typically "French" way (moss-green Louis XV and Louis XVI style, very much in fashion twenty years ago), the large cupboards and the particularly attentive staff will make you appreciate this hotel. This is a classic.

Résidence Bouquet de Longchamp ★★★

6 rue du Bouquet-de-Longchamp - 75016 Paris
Tel. : (1) 47 04 41 71 - Telex : 648 175 - Fax : (1) 47 27 29 09
Manager : Mr Tamzali

♦ *17 rooms with shower or bath, direct dial line, TV and minibar* ♦ *Prices : single : 545 F ; double : 595 F* ♦ *Breakfast with fresh orange juice : 33 F* ♦ *Credit cards : American Express, Diners and Visa* ♦ *Facilities : reservations, laundry, dry-cleaning* ♦ *No dogs allowed* ♦ *Parking facilities : 13 rue de Magdebourg* ♦ *Transportation : Metro stations Boissière, Trocadéro or Iéna, RER Charles-de-Gaulle-Etoile - Orly Airport bus : place de l'Etoile - Buses 22, 30, 32, 63, 72 and 82.*

Everything here is small : the street, the hotel (17 rooms !), the sitting room, the bedrooms. But it is all charming. Opposite stands a brick building built in the 1910s where each window is ornamented by a flowered ceramic plate, kitsch and original. The lobby is pleasant : all beige, from the leather sofas to the slightly ruffled curtains. A touch of green with a hedge of exotic plants decorate the bay giving on the street. The breakfast room is pretty and for once it is furnished in Louis XVI style, has no vault and shows a combination of ecru and watered material ; it leads to a light well where evergreen plants brighten up a blind wall. One colour also for the rooms, including the bathroom tiles : blue or ivory. True, they aren't large but easy to live in because the furniture matches the colour and size of the room.

St. James's Club **** L

5 place Chancelier-Adenauer - 75116 Paris
Tel. : (1) 47 04 29 29 - Telex : 643 850 - Fax : (1) 45 53 00 61
Manager : Mr Boone

*◆ 14 rooms, 34 suites and 2 air-conditioned pavilions with bath,
TV by satellite and video, hair-drier, safe and minibar, direct dial
line ◆ Garden, library-piano-bar, restaurants, conference room,
billiards room, health club, sauna ◆ Prices : single or double :
1 600 to 2 400 F ; suite : 2 850 to 7 450 F - Subscription as
temporary member : 50 F/day ◆ Breakfast : 100 F ◆ Credit
cards : American Express, Diners and Visa ◆ Facilities : all those
of its category, snacks, secretarial work and "Transpac" system
◆ Dogs allowed in the rooms ◆ Parking facilities : by carrier
◆ Transportation : Metro station Dauphine, RER and Roissy
Airport bus : Charles-de-Gaulle-Etoile - Buses PC, 52 and 82.*

In the evening, when the façade is illuminated in such light that
attracts the eye to the high chimneys, the St. James becomes like a
castle, at the edge of the Bois de Boulogne. In the daytime, it still is
a massive town house built by the widow of Thiers to be a
foundation for law students.
A cosy English style elegance for the lounge, the two restaurants
and the library-bar where wainscotting frames a sumptuous line of
leather bound books. The lines show a 1930s rigour. The rooms give
on private winter gardens or beautiful terraces. Obviously, the
bathrooms are princely. In the basement a health club, and a
billiards room.

La Villa Maillot ★★★★

143 avenue Malakoff - 75116 Paris
Tel. : (1) 45 01 25 22 - Telex : 649 808 - Fax : (1) 45 00 60 61
Manager : Mr Beherec

♦ *39 rooms and 3 suites, sound-proofed and air-conditioned, with bath, direct dial line, TV by satellite, hair-drier, trouser-press and minibar* ♦ *Bar, restaurant "Le Jardin", conference room* ♦ *Prices : single : 1 400 F ; double : 1 600 F ; suite : 2 100 and 2 300 F - Extra bed : 200 F* ♦ *Continental breakfast or buffet : 90 F* ♦ *Off-season : August* ♦ *Credit cards : American Express, Diners, Eurocard, JCB, MasterCard and Visa* ♦ *Facilities : all those of its category, secretarial work* ♦ *Dogs allowed* ♦ *Parking facilities : private garage in the hotel* ♦ *Transportation : Metro station Porte Maillot, RER Charles-de-Gaulle-Etoile - Roissy Airport bus : Porte Maillot - Buses PC, 73 and 82.*

This very sophisticated hotel is exactly what was needed to this business triangle formed by the Palais des Congrès, Neuilly and La Défense. It was inaugurated in 1988.

An appeasing luminosity pervades all over. The lounge-bar picutre windows which are open in summer give on a flowered winter garden ; a glass roof set in mirrors diffuses light over the fat sofas of sandy-coloured leather, light oak lead-white woodworks, sharp-lined furniture. Vertical windows frame the trees on the avenue. The universe of the large, cool and restful rooms is ivory or subtle grey, the beds are queen-size and there is a kitchenette so that you can have a snack in your room (but the breakfast-buffet is worth going downstairs : porridge, corn flakes, bacon and eggs, fruit and fresh fruit juices, compote : then you'll be ready for a good day !). Modern furniture is here for the comfort of a hard to please clientele. In the background an art deco decoration skillfully chosen, makes it very light and original.

Hôtel Cheverny ★★★

7 villa Berthier - 75017 Paris
Tel. : (1) 43 80 46 42 - Telex : 648 848 - Fax : (1) 47 63 26 62
Manager : Mr Gillot

♦ *50 rooms, sound-proofed on the street side, with shower or bath, direct dial line, TV by satellite, hair-drier, safe and minibar* ♦ *Patio, bar, conference rooms* ♦ *Prices : single with shower : 440 F, with bath : 460 F ; double with shower : 470 F, with bath : 500 and 540 F ; triple with bath : 690 F* ♦ *Breakfast : 35 F* ♦ *Off-season : August* ♦ *Credit cards : Air+, American Express, Diners, En Route and Visa* ♦ *Facilities : reservations, laundry, dry-cleaning* ♦ *No dogs allowed* ♦ *Parking facilities : 10 boulevard de l'Yser* ♦ *Transportation : Metro station Porte-de-Champerret, RER Porte Maillot - Roissy Airport bus : Porte Maillot - Buses PC, 83, 84 and 92.*

In less than a year, Mr Gillot has transformed a nice little district hotel into a very comfortable and performing establishment with 50 rooms. The next door building was annexed, the lobby enlarged and covered with marble, a vast basement floor was created where you'll find a bar, a lounge and conference rooms, and 32 of the rooms were arranged in today's fashion (pastel shades, soft lights and prints) with good bathrooms.

On each floor there are pretty sitting room corners. There, when the windows are open in the summer, you can take in the freshness and the fragrance of the patio down below.

Eighteen rooms only remain as they were in the old Hôtel Cheverny. Let's bet that the manager's gifts will quickly modernize them. A hotel which is now very competitive in this business area, and has found its own personality.

Hôtel de Banville ★★★

166 boulevard Berthier - 75017 Paris
Tel. : (1) 42 67 70 16 - Telex : 643 025 - Fax : (1) 44 40 42 77
Manager : Mrs d'Ambert

♦ *39 rooms with shower or bath, direct dial line, TV, hair-drier*
♦ *Bar* ♦ *Prices : single : 520 F ; double : 570 F - Extra bed :*
100 F ♦ *Breakfast : 35 F* ♦ *Off-season : 15 December to*
February and 15 July to 15 August ♦ *Credit cards : American*
Express, Eurocard, MasterCard and Visa ♦ *Facilities :*
reservations, laundry, dry-cleaning, snacks ♦ *Dogs allowed*
♦ *Parking facilities : 10 boulevard de l'Yser* ♦ *Transportation :*
Metro stations Pereire or Porte-de-Champerret - Roissy Airport
bus : Porte Maillot - Buses PC, 83, 84, 92 and 93.

We fell in love on sight with this 1930s building. The hotel kept the period glass gates, staircase and lift. Then it was classically furnished and every piece has its own place. Everything has charm, from the sitting room chintz curtains matching the dining room wallpaper, up to small objects : lamp, vase, mirror. A bar has just open, decorated in the same spirit. The rooms are alike. Of a good size, they give on the trees of the boulevard or on the neighbouring gardens. They are simple but charmingly furnished in bamboo and decorated with soft colours. A small armchair, round table and print calico curtains give character to each one. The seventh floor is higher than the surrounding roofs and from there the view is startling. This hotel is special, the rates are reasonnable and you are welcomed with an uncommon hospitality : the breakfast is a reference. Apart from the classic "continental" breakfast, there are two other formulas : "good shape" (60 F) with cold meats or eggs, cheese, corn flakes, yogurt and fruit, or "diet" with fresh fruit juice, wholesome bread, diet butter and yogurt...

Hôtel Etoile-Pereire ★★★

146 boulevard Pereire - 75017 Paris
Tel. : (1) 42 67 60 00 - Fax : (1) 42 67 02 90
Manager : Mr Pardi

♦ *21 rooms, 4 duplex apt. and 1 suite, sound-proofed, with shower or bath, direct dial line, TV (Canal+) and minibar* ♦ *Prices : single with shower : 460 F, with bath : 570 F ; double with bath : 650 F ; suite and duplex apt. : 900 F - Extra bed : 150 F* ♦ *Breakfast : 50 F* ♦ *Off-season : last 2 weeks of December and 15 July to 15 August* ♦ *Credit cards : American Express, Diners and Visa* ♦ *Facilities : reservations, laundry, dry-cleaning* ♦ *No dogs allowed* ♦ *Parking facilities : 42 rue Laugier and 30 rue Rennequin* ♦ *Transportation : Metro station and RER Pereire - Roissy Airport bus : Porte Maillot - Buses 43, 83, 84 and 92.*

This hotel is almost totally turned toward the courtyard (except the lobby and one room), this is no doubt an advantage in this area so close to the Porte Maillot. However, the boulevard Pereire was transformed into a garden by the City of Paris and thus took a residential appearance.

The refined neo-classic decoration is very welcoming. The lobby has beige marble floor and walls, brown sofas. The rooms are quite small but skillfully arranged and decorated in pastel colours : blue, sandy or apricot, enhanced by white bedspreads and flowered curtains. There is a pretty duplex apartment on the fourth floor.

A friendly welcome and a sumptuous breakfast with 24 different jams and jellies, Mr Pardi's pride.

Hôtel de Neuville ★★★

3 place Verniquet - 75017 Paris
Tel. : (1) 43 80 26 30 - Telex : 648 822 - Fax : (1) 43 80 38 55
Manager : Mr Bigeard

♦ *28 rooms, sound-proofed on the street side, with bath, TV, direct dial line* ♦ *Bar, tea-room, restaurant "Les Tartines" (closed on Saturdays and Sundays)* ♦ *Prices : single with bath : 540 F ; double : 595 to 630 F - Extra bed : 160 F* ♦ *Breakfast : 38 F* ♦ *Off-season : weekends and August* ♦ *Credit cards : American Express, Diners, Eurocard, MasterCard and Visa* ♦ *Facilities : reservations, laundry, dry-cleaning, snacks* ♦ *Dogs allowed* ♦ *Transportation : Metro stations Pereire or Wagram, RER Pereire - Roissy Airport bus : Porte Maillot - Buses 31, 53, 83, 84, 92, 93 and 94.*

At the corner of the boulevard Pereire, the white façade of this hotel erects its six floors on a tipically Napoléon III square. A few steps put the lobby, the living room and the bar at different levels ; a tiny patio brightens up the back wall framed by two neo-classic columns highlighting the beautiful space of the raised ground floor. On the whole it looks slightly Italian : sand colour, 1930s mat-brown armchairs, large terracotta pots overflowing with greenery and contemporary paintings... Sound-proofed, light, practical (enough closets ; always a table and two chairs), the rooms are very nice. Brass beds, flowered prints, and light wood furniture are in harmony with the pink or beige shades of the walls.
Remember the rooms bearing numbers in 5 or 6, bright and of a good size, they benefit from the view on the boulevard Pereire. Try the restaurant: the menu is tempting ! A pretty hotel, welcoming, managed by intelligent people.

Hôtel Regent's Garden ★★★

6 rue Pierre-Demours - 75017 Paris
Tel. : (1) 45 74 07 30 - Telex : 640 127 - Fax : (1) 40 55 01 42
Manager : Mr Frot

♦ *40 rooms with bath, direct dial line, cable TV, hair-drier and minibar* ♦ *Garden* ♦ *Prices : single : 580 F ; double : 620 F ; triple : 850 F* ♦ *Breakfast : 34 F* ♦ *Off-season : January and August* ♦ *Credit cards : American Express, Diners, Eurocard, MasterCard and Visa* ♦ *Facilities : reservations, laundry, dry-cleaning, snacks* ♦ *Dogs allowed* ♦ *Parking facilities : private garage in the hotel and 38 avenue des Ternes* ♦ *Transportation : Metro stations Ternes, Etoile or Porte Maillot, RER Charles-de-Gaulle-Etoile - Roissy Airport bus : Porte Maillot - Buses PC, 30, 31, 43 and 83.*

A porch surmounted by a tiled roof, a courtyard shaded by three big chestnut trees, a white house with sloping ceilings on the top floor, and hidden in the back, a garden, a real one with geraniums, lavender clumps, a fountain, love angels and a vask, enclosed by greenery growing freely. This house was built upon Napoleon III's request, for his physician. It is but a few minutes away from the Etoile or the Palais des Congrès. The charm is undeniable and you feel as if you were in another world. Some people may be slightly disappointed coming at the top of the porch steps leading to the vast sea-green lobby. In the rooms, the volumes, woodworks and the high windows are untouched ; but the fine taste which such a place deserves isn't there, this is even more obvious in the rooms giving on the garden or those on the top floors where so little is needed to make them delightful. The surroundings, a polite welcome... this could be an excellent hotel, unfortunately the uninteresting interior decoration slightly ruins it.

Hôtel Raphaël Paris ★★★★ L

17 avenue Kléber - 75116 Paris
Tel. : (1) 45 02 16 00 - Telex : 610 356 - Fax : (1) 45 01 21 50
Manager : Mr Astier

♦ *55 rooms and 28 suites, sound-proofed, with bath, direct dial line, TV and minibar ; air-conditioning in some rooms* ♦ *Bar, restaurant, conference and reception rooms with terrace* ♦ *Prices : single or double : 1 500 to 2 000 F ; suite : 2 000 to 3 600 F ; apartment : 4 500 to 6 000 F - Extra bed : 300 F* ♦ *Breakfast : 95 F* ♦ *Off-season : January and August* ♦ *Credit cards : American Express, Diners, Eurocard, MasterCard and Visa* ♦ *Facilities : all those of its category, secretarial work* ♦ *Dogs allowed* ♦ *Parking facilities : 8 avenue Foch* ♦ *Transportation : Metro station Kléber, RER and Roissy Airport bus : Charles-de-Gaulle-Etoile - Buses 22, 30, 31, 52, 54, 73 and 92.*

No word can be strong enough to express the quality of this hotel. We might as well say that it is the ultimate reference among Paris hotels because of its interior decoration as well as because of the service. Built in the 1920s to attract the high society clientele of the neighbouring Majestic, it personifies the refinement of that era. However, there is not one art deco object : the traditional clientele of that time would have been shocked. And what a decoration ! Flowered linen cloth, mirrors with painted woodwork frames, elegant furniture, alcoves hidden behind long curtains, wardrobes large enough to house a trunk, luminous bay windows. Comfortable bathrooms sometimes preceded by a boudoir closed by damask curtains. The rooms are as large as lounges, the suites are like ballrooms. The English bar is one of the most pleasant in all Paris. The staff is concerned, attentive and obliging. You can feel ill at ease in this slightly nostalgic hotel, as for us, it is splendid.

Hôtel du Bois ★★

11 rue du Dôme - 75116 Paris
Tel. : (1) 45 00 31 96 - Telex : 615 453 - Fax : (1) 45 00 90 05
Manager : Mr Byrne

♦ *41 sound-proofed rooms with shower or bath, direct dial line, TV and minibar* ♦ *No lift* ♦ *Prices : single with shower : 385 F ; double with shower or bath : 465 to 535 F - Extra bed : 100 F* ♦ *Breakfast with orange juice : included* ♦ *Off-season : January, February, 15 July to 31 August and Christmas* ♦ *Credit cards : American Express and Visa* ♦ *Facilities : reservations* ♦ *Dogs allowed* ♦ *Parking facilities : 8 avenue Foch and 2 rue Lauriston* ♦ *Transportation : Metro stations Kléber or Charles-de-Gaulle-Etoile, RER and Roissy Airport bus : Charles-de-Gaulle-Etoile - Buses 22, 30, 31, 52, 73 and 92.*

The Hôtel du Bois is like Montmartre at the Etoile, and England in Paris!
Montmartre because you must climb steep stairs from the place Victor Hugo to arrive to the small rue du Dôme, England because everything here evoques this country : from the curtains and the paisley patterns, to the lamps diffusing intimate light, impressionistes posters in the corridors, fresh rooms with flowery prints of sweet colours, and the welcome, delicious.
Do we have to add that Mr Byrne is an Englishman?
And last but not least, the very unexpensive bill in such an area will make indecisive people run to it.

Hôtel Alexander ★★★★

102 avenue Victor-Hugo - 75116 Paris
Tel. : (1) 45 53 64 65 - Telex : 610 373 - Fax : (1) 45 53 12 51
Manager : Mr Cartier

♦ *60 rooms and 2 suites, sound-proofed on the street side, with shower or bath, direct dial line, TV, hair-drier and minibar* ♦ *Prices : single with shower or bath : 760 to 990 F ; double with bath : 925 to 1 035 F ; suite : 1 870 F - Extra bed : 200 F* ♦ *Breakfast : 55 F* ♦ *Off-season : 15 July to 30 August* ♦ *Credit cards : American Express, Diners, Eurocard, MasterCard and Visa* ♦ *Facilities : all those of its category, snacks* ♦ *No dogs allowed* ♦ *Parking facilities : opposite 122 avenue Victor-Hugo* ♦ *Transportation : Metro station Victor-Hugo, RER and Roissy Airport bus : Charles-de-Gaulle-Etoile - Buses 30, 32, 52 and 82.*

The superb light woodworks add a touch of warmth to the ground floor and give the key note to this small 4-star hotel : intimate elegance ; dark studded flooring, and further on a beautiful moquette showing a floral pattern. The furnishing is simple straw yellow velvet Louis XV or modern. Throughout the hotel you'll see a large mirror, beautiful bracket lamps, a fine console ; several well proportioned sitting rooms thus follow one another. Here, the ultimate comfort is space, offered in the rooms with as much generosity. Therefore, all of them are particularly agreeable, even the "smaller" ones : their cupboards and wardrobes deserve their names, the bathrooms are often big enough to lodge a dressing table. Papered with light-coloured flowers, carefully furnished in 18th century style, the back rooms are most pleasant for they look out onto the neighbouring gardens. Traditional, in the best meaning of the word, the rates are quite reasonnable for a hotel of this category.

Résidence Chambellan-Morgane ★★★

6 rue Keppler - 75116 Paris
Tel. : (1) 47 20 35 72 - Telex : 613 682 - Fax : (1) 47 20 95 69
Manager : Mrs Nicol

♦ *20 sound-proofed rooms with shower or bath, direct dial line, TV, hair-drier and minibar* ♦ *Prices : single or double with shower : 540 F, with bath : 720 F, with bath and sitting room corner : 810 F* ♦ *Breakfast with orange juice : 40 F* ♦ *Off-season : last 2 weeks of December and August* ♦ *Credit cards : American Express, Diners, Eurocard and Visa* ♦ *Facilities : reservations, laundry, dry-cleaning* ♦ *No dogs allowed* ♦ *Parking facilities : opposite 103 avenue des Champs-Elysées and 47 rue de Chaillot* ♦ *Transportation : Metro station, RER and Roissy Airport bus : Charles-de-Gaulle-Etoile - Buses 22, 30, 31, 32, 52, 73 and 92.*

The porch and the entrance hall of this new hotel are like a 18th century theatre where scenes between shephards and shephardesses could be acted. It is entirely decorated in pink Louis XVI style, from the vestibule with fine ornamental mouldings to the corridors and the large lounge with rounded bays. In this omnipresent pink, only the chairs and armchairs, the moquettes covering the corridors are blue.

This candy-like atmosphere is also found in the rooms covered with watered wallpapers, delicately flowered calico and furnished in a modern style with light wooden pieces tinted light blue or beige. This is Sleeping Beauty's castle to which the Franco-Italian jabber of Raphaël, the factotum, gives life.

ETOILE - CHAMPS-ELYSEES

Hôtel Centre-Ville Etoile ★★★

6 rue des Acacias - 75017 Paris
Tel. : (1) 43 80 56 18 - Telex : 650 343 - Fax : (1) 47 54 93 43
Manager : Mr Michaud

♦ *20 rooms, sound-proofed on street side, with bath, direct dial line, TV by satellite, safe, minibar and individual air-conditioning* ♦ *Restaurant "Le Cougar" (closed at lunch time on Saturdays and on Sundays)* ♦ *Prices : single or double : 1 000 F - Extra bed : 150 F* ♦ *Breakfast with fresh orange juice and cheese : 50 F* ♦ *Off-season : November, December and August* ♦ *Credit cards : American Express, Diners and Visa* ♦ *Facilities : reservations, laundry, dry-cleaning, snacks* ♦ *Dogs allowed* ♦ *Parking facilities : 24 rue des Acacias* ♦ *Transportation : Metro stations Argentine or Charles-de-Gaulle-Etoile, RER and Roissy Airport bus : Charles-de-Gaulle-Etoile - Buses 22, 30, 31, 43, 52, 73 and 92.*

Originally, this was an uninteresting brick building standing on the corner between a street and a passageway. A high glass wall with a metallic structure stands in front of the U shaped façade. This has given it a look and character it never had before. The space thus gained was used to create a lobby, the ancient outside galleries were transformed into corridors leading to the rooms. Then, in a game between lines and tranparence, black and white, the hotel was renovated in a really modern style.

The rooms are still small but acquired a personal charm : white walls (recalled by the white stitched cotton bedspreads), black furniture, a white rug with fine black stripes. A 1930 touch with the armchairs, bracket lamps and bathrooms, small of course, but ravishing, they are entirely white with a fine black frieze or covered with grey mosaics reflected in a mirror wall.

ETOILE - CHAMPS-ELYSEES

Etoile-Park Hôtel ★★★

10 avenue Mac-Mahon - 75017 Paris
Tel. : (1) 42 67 69 63 - Telex : 649 266 - Fax : (1) 43 80 18 99
Manager : Mr Dian

♦ *28 sound-proofed rooms with shower or bath, direct dial line, cable TV, hair-drier, safe and minibar* ♦ *Prices : single with shower : 435 F, with bath : 595 F ; double with bath : 620 to 690 F - Extra bed : 100 F* ♦ *Breakfast (buffet) : 45 F ; American breakfast : 65 F* ♦ *Off-season : January and August* ♦ *Credit cards : American Express, Diners and Visa* ♦ *Facilities : reservations, laundry, dry-cleaning* ♦ *Dogs allowed* ♦ *Parking facilities : 24 rue des Acacias* ♦ *Transportation : Metro station, RER and Roissy Airport bus : Charles-de-Gaulle-Etoile - Buses 22, 30, 31, 52, 73 and 92.*

This is another hotel falling for the charm of the 1930s, and this with a certain elegance. Some people may find the modern sharpness slightly cold, but it doesn't show at once : a bright-red marble desk brightens the beige and grey colours of the lobby. Around the bar, beautiful armchairs in sycamore wood complete this luminous and refined space.

Most of the rooms are small (except two on the top floor) but are also sophisticated. Maybe too much so : beautiful black furniture, subtle beige and grey moquette, bedspreads and wallcoverings, with an adjoined immaculate bathroom, all this lacks the warmth of softer lines. The atmosphere of the rooms is almost sad. Too bad, because not much would be needed to enliven them. A pretty place, slightly formal...

92

Hôtel Tilsitt-Etoile ★★★

23 rue Brey - 75017 Paris
Tel. : (1) 43 80 39 71 - Telex : 640 629 - Fax : (1) 47 66 37 63
Managers : Mrs Cot and Mrs Lafosse

♦ *39 sound-proofed rooms with shower or bath, direct dial line, TV, hair-drier and minibar* ♦ *Bar, conference room* ♦ *Prices : single : 520 to 600 F ; double with bath : 650 F ; junior-suite : 800 F - Extra bed : 100 F* ♦ *Breakfast with fruit juice : 35 F* ♦ *Off-season : 15 July to 20 August* ♦ *Credit cards : American Express, Diners and Visa* ♦ *Facilities : reservations, laundry, dry-cleaning, snacks* ♦ *Small dogs allowed* ♦ *Parking facilities : FNAC car park, avenue de Wagram* ♦ *Transportation : Metro stations Ternes or Etoile, RER Charles-de-Gaulle-Etoile - Buses 22, 30, 31, 43, 52, 73, 83 and 92.*

A few hotels located between Etoile and Ternes raised with talent the average of the area. The Tilsitt is one of them and it has many qualities : calm, elegance, and a sense of welcome.

We liked the way Mrs Lafosse and Mrs Cot played with space, levels and colours to create a place where you immediately feel at home.

From the living room-bar with a fresh and intimate corner – where grey is hightened by several mirrors, colourful paintings and the light coming out of the tiny patio – up to the rooms, all of a good size and comfortable, peaceful with their shades of grey or beige hightened with prints of more vivid colours. Refined bathrooms, completely white, set in beige or grey depending on the room.

Very good service. A place to come back to.

Hôtel Eber-Monceau ★★★

18 rue Léon-Jost - 75017 Paris
Tel. : (1) 46 22 60 70 - Telex : 649 949 - Fax : (1) 47 63 01 01
Manager : Mr Eber

♦ *13 rooms, 3 suites and 2 duplex apt. with shower or bath, direct dial line, cable TV, hair-drier and minibar* ♦ *Small patio, bar* ♦ *Prices : single or double : 550 to 600 F ; suite : 950 F ; duplex apt. : 1 200 F* ♦ *Breakfast with orange juice : 40 F* ♦ *Off-season : August* ♦ *Credit cards : American Express, Diners, Eurocard, MasterCard and Visa* ♦ *Facilities : reservations, laundry, dry-cleaning* ♦ *No dogs allowed* ♦ *Parking facilities : 100 rue de Courcelles* ♦ *Transportation : Metro station Courcelles, RER and Roissy Airport bus : Charles-de-Gaulle-Etoile - Buses 30, 31, 84 and 94.*

A true character born from the freedom of the decorative style. First of all, you'll notice the high wooden fireplace Henri II, then the painted beams, Renaissance style. Second, come the cane English armchairs, pink marble flooring, the 1930s bar brightened by a patio where some chairs are set in summer. All this is a real success.

You'll stop in the bluish grey corridors to look at curious engravings showing how the Statue of Liberty was built in Bartholdi's studio, in the nearby rue de Chazelles. The rooms are slightly disappointing. Small, in faded beige and grey colours, they are less engaging. However, except the too heavy wardrobes, the furniture is pretty : 19th century, 1930s or modern, chosen with taste and well proportioned... The spacious and luminous duplex apartments would be perfect but for their price, even if you take into account the hotel's excellent facilities ! The bathrooms are beautiful : entirely white, except for the little frieze running around the wall and the earth-coloured floor tiles.

Hôtel Atala ★★★★

10 rue Chateaubriand - 75008 Paris
Tel. : (1) 45 62 01 62 - Telex : 640 576 - Fax : (1) 42 25 66 38
Manager : Mr Tolub

♦ *47 rooms and 2 apartments, sound-proofed and air-conditioned, with bath, direct dial line, TV by satellite and minibar* ♦ *Garden, bar, restaurant* ♦ *Prices : single : 750 to 950 F ; double : 950 to 1 250 F ; apartment : 1 250 F - Extra bed : 150 F* ♦ *Breakfast with fruit juice : 45 F* ♦ *Off-season : December, January, July and August* ♦ *Credit cards : American Express, Diners, Eurocard, MasterCard and Visa* ♦ *Facilities : reservations, laundry, dry-cleaning, snacks* ♦ *Dogs allowed* ♦ *Parking facilities : George-V car park, opposite 103 avenue des Champs-Elysées* ♦ *Transportation : Metro station George-V, RER and Roissy Airport bus : Charles-de-Gaulle-Etoile - Buses 22, 30, 31, 43, 52, 73 and 92.*

A garden with tall trees and a quiet street so close to the place de l'Etoile are uncommon assets, and the Atala makes use of them with great simplicity. There is no excess in the decoration of this 4-star hotel which high façade with stone balustrades built in the 1930s stands erect in the quiet rue Chateaubriand : the large volumes were judiciously used. The restaurant takes most of it, it opens onto the garden's clumps of hydrangeas; in the afternoon it becomes a sitting room where one sits with pleasure. Dark wainscoting, long curtains printed with bamboos, comfortable furniture, all this decoration favours an art of living. Mr Tolub's practical sense also shows in the rooms, large enough to integrate a sitting room corner. Long tables, cosy armchairs, lights ; and as a background to the burr elm furniture, a carefully designed harmony of beige and brown. Spacious bathrooms, well equipped. On the eighth floor, the rooms have balconies and a view on the Sacré-Cœur, the golden dome of the Invalides, the Eiffel Tower...

Résidence Lord Byron ★★★

5 rue Chateaubriand - 75008 Paris
Tel. : (1) 43 59 89 98 - Telex : 649 662 - Fax : (1) 42 89 46 04
Manager : Mrs Coisne-Benoit

♦ *31 rooms with shower or bath, direct dial line, TV and safe, (minibar in some rooms)* ♦ *Flowered courtyard* ♦ *Prices : single : 530 to 670 F ; double : 670 to 770 F ; suite : 1 100 F - Extra bed : 170 F* ♦ *Breakfast : 45 F* ♦ *Off-season : last 2 weeks of December* ♦ *Credit cards : Eurocard, MasterCard and Visa* ♦ *Facilities : reservations, laundry, dry-cleaning* ♦ *No dogs allowed* ♦ *Parking facilities : 5 rue de Berri and opposite 103 avenue des Champs-Elysées* ♦ *Transportation : Metro stations George-V or Charles-de-Gaulle-Etoile, RER and Roissy Airport bus : Charles-de-Gaulle-Etoile - Buses 22, 52, 73 and 92.*

Flowers and lights everywhere. Several bouquets stand under the lantern brightening the ivory-coloured vestibule, rounded bays, steps go up to the lobby and further, to the lounge, furnished in Louis XVI style (blue velvet and crystal chandelier). In the courtyard, where you can have breakfast or tea in summertime : jars, primroses and a pavilion in the back. In the rooms papered in pink, blue or flowered wallpaper, the curtains and bedspreads are strewn with spring bouquets or giant tropical flowers. They are soft, luminous and classic, adjoined to white bathrooms. Our favourites : the fifth and sixth floor rooms with sloping ceilings and the large ones with a sitting room corner ; finally those on the ground floor in the pavilion between two gardens...

Within a stone's throw from the Etoile, this is a pretty hotel benefiting from a quiet street and the surrounding interior gardens.

Hôtel Balzac ★★★★

6 rue Balzac - 75008 Paris
Tel. : (1) 45 61 97 22 - Telex : 290 298 - Fax : (1) 42 25 24 82
Manager : Mr Falcucci

◆ *56 rooms and 14 suites, sound-proofed and air-conditioned, with bath, direct dial line, TV, hair-drier and minibar* ◆ *Bar, Italian restaurant "Bice", conference rooms* ◆ *Prices : single : 1 460 F ; double 1 680 F ; suite : 3 000 to 3 500 F - Extra bed : 250 F* ◆ *Breakfast with fresh fruit juice and fruit : 85 F* ◆ *Off-season : December, January, July and August* ◆ *Credit cards : American Express, Diners and Visa* ◆ *Facilities : all those of its category, snacks, secretarial work* ◆ *Small dogs allowed* ◆ *Parking facilities : by carrier and George-V car park, opposite 103 avenue des Champs-Elysées* ◆ *Transportation : Metro stations Charles-de-Gaulle-Etoile or George-V, RER and Roissy Airport bus : Charles-de-Gaulle-Etoile - Buses 22, 30, 31, 32, 52, 73 and 92.*

Very close to the place de l'Etoile, the Balzac has become very attractive behind its façade built at the end of the last century, since its renovation which obviously shows taste in the arrangement of the space and the choice of materials. The heightened ground floor is organized on different levels which surround a large lounge lit by a glass roof, this is a strategic place leading to smaller lounges, a circular conference room, the restaurant and the bar... Period pieces, oriental rugs, ancient wall lamps, cupolas and glass partitions, moquette with a geometrical pattern, sharply designed sofas and chairs stand according to an organized stage set, where one is attracted by today's decorative game at once classical and modern. In the rooms – decorated in warm shades – American comfort : large space, king-size beds, fluffy moquette, satin-like materials. Very bright, large marble bathrooms where you'll find cosy bathrobes. Very good service, garanteed serenity.

Hôtel de Vigny ★★★★

9-11 rue Balzac - 75008 Paris
Tél. : (1) 40 75 04 39 - Fax : (1) 40 75 05 81
Direction : Mr Falcucci

♦ *25 rooms and 12 suites, sound-proofed and air-conditioned, with bath, 2 direct dial lines, cable TV and Canal+, hair-drier, safe and minibar ; hi-fi system and jacuzzi in the suites* ♦ *"Baretto", piano bar* ♦ *Prices : single : 1 500 F ; double : 1 700 to 1 900 F ; suite : from 2 000 F* ♦ *Continental or English breakfast : from 90 F* ♦ *Credit cards : American Express, Diners and Visa* ♦ *Facilities : those of its category, snacks* ♦ *No dogs allowed* ♦ *Parking facilities : 50 spaces in the hotel* ♦ *Transportation : Metro station, RER and Orly Airport bus : Charles-de-Gaulle-Etoile - Buses 22, 30, 31, 52, 73 and 92.*

This hotel which has just opened is a master stroke of the American company which already owns the Balzac. More than a hotel, a residence. With reminiscences of "old England" seductions, and French decorative virtuosity...

The rooms are all different ; you go, with brilliance and tact, from warm tartans and flannels to delicate tints in a Restauration or Napoléon III styles, through spaces of extreme comfort.

Panelling and wooden fireplace, ginger-coloured prints, mahogany furniture and large sofas make the large living room punctuated by four neo-classic, round columns – superb. In a corner, as if it were forgotten, a very pretty cabinet from the 17th century.

Sumptuous but nonetheless intimist, the hotel demonstrates of a perfect art of living from the bar, very nice, to the refined breakfasts.

Hôtel Vernet ★★★★

25 rue Vernet - 75008 Paris
Tel. : (1) 47 23 43 10 - Telex : 290 347 - Fax : (1) 40 70 10 14
Manager : Mr Lechénet

♦ *54 rooms and 3 suites, sound-proofed and air-conditioned, with shower or bath, direct dial line, cable* TV *and Canal+, minibar ; jacuzzi in rooms with bath* ♦ *Bar, restaurant, free access to the "Thermes" (fitness club of the Royal-Monceau)* ♦ *Price : single with shower : 1 350 F, with bath : 1 600 F ; double with bath : 1 600 to 1 850 F ; suite : 2 700 F - Extra bed : 250 F* ♦ *Breakfast with fresh orange juice : 90 F ; American breakfast : 120 F* ♦ *Off-season : 15 July to 31 August* ♦ *Credit cards : American Express, Diners and Visa* ♦ *Facilities : all those of its category, snacks* ♦ *Dogs allowed* ♦ *Parking facilities : George-V car park, opposite 103 avenue des Champs-Elysées* ♦ *Transportation : Metro station, RER and Orly Airport bus : Charles-de-Gaulle-Etoile - Buses 22, 30, 31, 52, 73 and 92.*

Traditional up to the awning of the entrance, the Hôtel Vernet has managed to keep all its lustre to a decor of marble, mirrors, precious rugs and large picture windows. However, it can be surprising : a sumptuous glass roof conceived by Eiffel surmounts the imposing dining room, and a beautiful transparent lift climbing silently.

The rooms also, are classic, but who would complain about that when classicism means comfort, beautiful materials (fluffy moquette and flowery quilted bedspreads), and 19th century furniture. A cosy bar, entirely panelled, made in 1945, with many equestrian etchings from the 19th century by the painter Vernet. Don't forget a good gourmet restaurant.

Hôtel Centre-Ville Matignon ★★★

3 rue de Ponthieu - 75008 Paris
Tel. : (1) 42 25 73 01 - Telex : 650 343 - Fax : (1) 42 56 01 39
Manager : Mr Michaud

♦ *23 sound-proofed rooms and suites with bath, direct dial line, TV by satellite, hair-drier and minibar* ♦ *Bar, restaurant "Le Café Matignon"* ♦ *Prices : single or double : 1 000 F ; suite : 1 500 F - Extra bed : 100 F* ♦ *Breakfast included* ♦ *Off-season : winter (exclusive of professional shows)* ♦ *Credit cards : American Express, Diners, JCB and Visa* ♦ *Facilities : reservations, laundry, dry-cleaning, snacks* ♦ *Dogs allowed* ♦ *Parking facilities : 2 avenue Matignon and rue de Ponthieu* ♦ *Transportation : Metro station Franklin-Roosevelt, RER Charles-de-Gaulle-Etoile - Buses 28, 32, 42, 49, 52, 73, 80 and 83.*

The 1920s and 1930s are in fashion and many hotels were renovated in this spirit. However, this one is a bit special : extremely 1930s, the decoration is entirely genuine and this is excindingly rare. From the black and straw yellow mosaic over the hallway floor, to the door knobs and the mirrors engraved with tree leaves hung inside the lift, everything is authentic. Renovated in order to keep this atmosphere, this hotel lately reopened and is the third member of the group Centre-Ville. It is a remarkable success. A dark-red carpet with a black edge goes upstairs and around the storeys. In almost all the rooms, at the head of the bed, there is a genuine fresco showing a landscape. The furniture is modern but does not cheat the spirit of the place. The bathrooms are superb and original : yellow with a blue edge, most of them still have their genuine tiles, mosaics and gorgeous washstands. Of course they are impeccable. This is definitely what you can call a hotel with character... to be found even in the "homemade jams" at breakfast and in the final bill... expensive !

Hôtel Bradford ★★★

10 rue Saint-Philippe-du-Roule - 75008 Paris
Tel. : (1) 43 59 24 20 - Telex : 648 530 - Fax : (1) 45 63 20 07
Managers : Mr and Mrs Mourot

♦ *48 rooms with shower or bath, direct dial line and* TV ♦ *Prices : single with shower or bath : 600 F ; double : 700 F* ♦ *Breakfast included* ♦ *Off-season : 15 July to 15 August* ♦ *Credit cards : Visa* ♦ *Facilities : reservations, laundry, dry-cleaning* ♦ *No dogs allowed* ♦ *Transportation : Metro station Saint-Philippe-du-Roule - Buses 28, 32, 49, 52, 80 and 83.*

Nothing attracts the eye in this hotel located at the corner of two quiet streets not far from the Champs-Elysées, except an immaculate façade and a kind of conservative side to it which shall no doubt call the interest of onlookers and initiated.

Conservative ? Yes, and that's good when, as it is the case here, it means a respect of ancient qualities for both welcome and service, attentive and always smiling (Mr and Mrs Mourot have had the same staff for many years and this is always a good sign) ; or when it implies that the rooms newly painted have supreme comfort : space.

Aunthentic 1920s decoration, brass beds, outdated dressing tables and such practicle wardrobes, flowered curtains, velvet-like moquette and impeccable bathrooms, covered with light-grey marble for the new ones. Choose, if you can, the rooms whose numbers end with 6 or 7, truly big and at the same price,or those on the sixth floor, charming, or those, on the courtyard side, giving on the trees of the Canadian Embassy.

Living room and dining room with slightly stiff chairs and showing no genious, but a bunch of flowers at the entrance which is like the reception : magnificent.

Hôtel des Champs-Elysées ★★

2 rue d'Artois - 75008 Paris
Tel. : (1) 43 59 11 42 - Fax : (1) 45 61 00 61
Managers : Mr and Mrs Delfau

♦ *36 sound-proofed rooms with shower or bath, direct dial line, TV, hair-drier, safe and minibar* ♦ *Prices : single or double : 400 to 470 F - Extra bed : 80 F* ♦ *Breakfast : 28 F* ♦ *Off-season : August* ♦ *Credit card : Visa* ♦ *Facilities : reservations, laundry, dry-cleaning* ♦ *No dogs allowed* ♦ *Transportation : Metro station Saint-Philippe-du-Roule - Buses 28, 32, 49, 52, 80 and 83.*

A good 2-star in such a district, that is luck. Especially when people don't take advantage of a renovation to raise their rates.

Mr and Mrs Delfau, who are taking over a family business, wanted, and it is a success, a comfortable and charming arrangement, which is much better in many ways than what you expect from a 2-star.

The living room shows two tendancies : contemporary space on the street side, with good black leather sofas ; and "winter garden", on the side of the bar and the glass roof, with multicoloured wicker armchairs, a lot of greenery and a picture showing the avenue des Champs-Elysées.

Good feeling in the rooms, never too small, furnished with tinted burr elm (pink, ginger or grey), with pretty prints for the curtains and bedspreads. The bathrooms are well equipped, covered with big black tiles, grey or pinkish beige marble.

A very performing hotel where you'll be welcomed with care.

Hôtel de l'Elysée ★★★

12 rue des Saussaies - 75008 Paris
Tel. : (1) 42 65 29 25 - Telex : 281 665 - Fax : (1) 42 65 64 28
Manager : Mrs Lafond

♦ *30 rooms and 2 suites, sound-proofed, with shower or bath, direct dial line, TV and hair-drier ; air-conditioning in the suites* ♦ *Bar* ♦ *Prices : single or double with shower : 480 to 580 F, with bath : 650 to 880 F ; suite : 980 to 1 450 F* ♦ *Breakfast with fresh orange juice : 50 F* ♦ *Off-season : December and August* ♦ *Credit cards : American Express, Diners, JCB and Visa* ♦ *Facilities : reservations, laundry, dry-cleaning* ♦ *No dogs allowed* ♦ *Parking facilities : place de la Madeleine* ♦ *Transportation : Metro stations Miromesnil or Champs-Elysées-Clémenceau - Buses 22, 28, 32, 49, 52, 80 and 84.*

Within a stone's throw from the Faubourg-Saint-Honoré, and near the Champs-Elysées, this hotel was recently renovated with a virtuosity which can only be admired.

The vestibule and stairway are decorated in a soft green and beige marble trompe-l'œil, a true masterpiece. Pink or pale yellow, most of the rooms are furnished in Restauration style, they are models for tentativeness. The other rooms, furnished in Louis XVI style, are like Persia : prints showing birds or flowers now cover the walls, are now used as curtains or bedspreads. The chairs are in varnished cherry wood or painted in a greyish blue. In the rooms, you will find alcoves, tester beds or canopies. On the other hand, the modern bathrooms are uniformly perfect. The 2 suites with sloping ceilings on the sixth floor are exquisite. The rooms whose number ends with 1 or 4 present another asset : their size. A hotel whose refinement is incredible.

Hôtel San Régis ★★★★

12 rue Jean-Goujon - 75008 Paris
Tel. : (1) 43 59 41 90 - Telex : 643 637 - Fax : (1) 45 61 05 48
Manager : Mr Georges

♦ *34 rooms and 10 suites, sound-proofed and air-conditioned, with shower or bath, direct dial line, TV by satellite, hair-drier and minibar* ♦ *Bar, restaurant* ♦ *Prices : single : 1 250 to 1 420 F ; double : 1 850 to 2 100 F ; suite : 2 200 to 4 600 F - Extra bed : 200 F* ♦ *Breakfast : 90 F* ♦ *No off-season* ♦ *Credit cards : American Express, Diners and Visa* ♦ *Facilities : all those of its category, snacks* ♦ *No dogs allowed* ♦ *Parking facilities : by carrier and rue François-Ier* ♦ *Transportation : Metro station Franklin-D-Roosevelt, RER Charles-de-Gaulle-Etoile - Invalides air terminal - Buses 28, 42, 49, 73, 83 and 93.*

An awning and two lanterns show the hotel in this quiet street linking the Alma to the Grand Palais, and passing through an area where everything is prestigious – gardens, museums, theatres, restaurants, fashion designers... Tradition (the hotel exists since 1923), privacy (44 rooms only, and 10 suites), this beautiful 4-star is the expression of an art of living where French elegance and English comfort are united. Light oak wainscoting and draped chintz curtains, period furniture and woolen sofas, delicat china, ancient rugs over modern moquette : from one lounge to another and from the lobby to the rooms, everything is refined and warm. The bathrooms are just perfect : large and well lit ; arranged like boudoirs, with wallpaper and marble matching the rooms, a pretty table and a chair. Breakfast trays are good and the restaurant's menu, classic. Except the small, less expensive rooms, too ordinary for such a pretty place, this hotel is really exceptional.

Hôtel Franklin-Roosevelt ★★★

18 rue Clément-Marot - 75008 Paris
Tel. : (1) 47 23 61 66 - Telex : 614 797 - Fax : (1) 47 20 44 30
Manager : Mrs Prudhon

♦ *45 sound-proofed rooms with shower or bath, direct dial line, TV, hair-drier* ♦ *Prices : single with shower : 640 F, with bath : 720 F ; double with shower : 680 F, with bath : 760 F* ♦ *Breakfast included* ♦ *Off-season : 15 December to 8 January and August* ♦ *Credit cards : American Express and Visa* ♦ *Facilities : reservations, laundry, dry-cleaning, snacks* ♦ *No dogs allowed* ♦ *Parking facilities : George-V car park, opposite 103 avenue des Champs-Elysées and rue François-Ier* ♦ *Transportation : Metro stations Franklin-D-Roosevelt or Alma-Marceau, RER Charles-de-Gaulle-Etoile - Buses 32, 42, 63, 80 and 92.*

One can be deceived by appearances : who would have known that behind the slightly heavy façade of this 19th century building were hiding some of the most beautiful rooms we were to discover this year ? Rooms showing inspiration, starting with a naïve painting or sights painted directly on the wall, it leads us to a paradise out of "Paul and Virginie". Some furniture with light shapes, a bamboo frieze running along the ceiling, white cotton fabrics and the magic works. If you aren't lucky enough to be in one of those rooms you'll be nonetheless happy in the oriental-like, or very classic ones, black wooden furniture and caned wallpaper. All the rooms are spacious, they have excellent wardrobes and extremely comfortable bathrooms, some of them, newly renovated, with white or beige tiles, are just perfect. Thoughtful welcome and services, a very well managed hotel, but this runs in the family : Mrs Prudhon's ancestor is no other than Mr Tabary, who opened the restaurant "La Cascade".

Hôtel Queen Mary ★★★

9 rue Greffulhe - 75008 Paris
Tel. : (1) 42 66 40 50 - Telex : 640 419 - Fax : (1) 42 66 94 92
Manager : Mr Jaouen

♦ *36 rooms with shower or bath, direct dial line, TV, hair-drier and minibar* ♦ *Prices : single : 500 to 600 F ; double : 600 to 700 F ; triple : 850 F ; suite : 1 400 F* ♦ *Breakfast : 35 F* ♦ *Off-season : August* ♦ *Credit cards : Eurocard, MasterCard and Visa* ♦ *Facilities : reservations, laundry, dry-cleaning* ♦ *Dogs allowed* ♦ *Parking facilities : place de la Madeleine* ♦ *Transportation : Metro stations Madeleine or Havre-Caumartin, RER Auber - Buses 22, 24, 28, 32, 49, 80, 84 and 94.*

The rue Greffulhe hides Napoleon III town houses away from the bustling place de la Madeleine and the Grands Boulevards. One of the most typical shelters the Queen Mary. Its white façade is ornamented with an elegant awning, an elaborate gate flanked by two lanterns and a ravishing balcony. Inside, the decoration is traditional Louis XVI style. The lobby is pale blue, unexpectedly luminous and on each side there is a sitting room, one is pink, the other one blue. Nothing could be more classic : gilt bronze bracket lamps, crystal chandeliers, woodworks and a blue and beige moquette. The rooms are alike, in blue or faded yellow nuances. A narrow alcove at the head of the bed was made into a wardrobe, the furniture is comfortable. The management is renovating the bathrooms ; it's a shame for, although slightly old-fashioned, they were tiled with blue, green or yellow ceramic and the bathtub was sometimes placed in an alcove. They had a lot of character. The large rooms on the street side are the more agreeable, and on each floor two rooms communicate, thus forming a suite. One word about the welcome : obliging...

Hôtel Concortel ★★★

19-21 rue Pasquier - 75008 Paris
Tel. : (1) 42 65 45 44 - Telex : 660 228 - Fax : (1) 42 65 18 33
Manager : Mr Cenreaud

♦ *46 rooms and suites with shower or bath, direct dial line, TV, safe and minibar* ♦ *Bar, conference room* ♦ *Prices : single : 500 F ; double : 540 to 640 F ; suite : 740 F - Extra bed : 100 F* ♦ *Breakfast with cheese : 30 F* ♦ *Off-season : Christmas and New Year period, August* ♦ *Credit cards : American Express, Diners and Visa* ♦ *Facilities : reservations, laundry, dry-cleaning* ♦ *Dogs allowed* ♦ *Parking facilities : place de la Madeleine* ♦ *Transportation : Metro stations Madeleine or Havre-Caumartin, RER Auber - Buses 22, 24, 28, 32, 49, 80, 84 and 94.*

In a street which becomes quiet in the evening, the Concortel is a haven of comfort and peace. The first thing you'll notice after the salmon-pink and sea-green lobby is the moquette : little blue and faded red patterns draw big lozenges forming a kind of Oriental rug which covers the floor up to the doors of the rooms. These are classic and, as an exceptional comfort, all are quite large. Often, space was provided for an alcove which has a wardrobe on one side and opens on a marble or white tiled bathroom on the other. We recommend the 5 suites giving on the courtyard and benefiting from true silence and the comfort of a large wardrobe ; the large front rooms bearing numbers in 1 have two windows and a sofa. However this hotel's masterpiece is apartment #62, in the attic : a large room with sloping ceilings gives on a balcony and opens to the sky, it is luminous and calm, unfortunately never free, but it isn't more expensive for all that ! The organization and management of this hotel shows the rare quality of generosity.

Hôtel Lido ★★★

4 passage de la Madeleine - 75008 Paris
Tel. : (1) 42 66 27 37 - Telex : 281 039 - Fax : (1) 42 66 61 23
Manager : Mrs Teil

♦ *32 rooms with bath, direct dial line, cable* TV, *hair-drier, safe and minibar* ♦ *Prices : single : 600 to 650 F ; double : 700 to 750 F - Extra bed : 100 F* ♦ *Breakfast included* ♦ *Off-season : December to 15 January and August* ♦ *Credit cards : American Express, Diners, JCB and Visa* ♦ *Facilities : reservations, laundry, dry-cleaning* ♦ *Dogs allowed* ♦ *Parking facilities : place de la Madeleine and rue Chauveau-Lagarde* ♦ *Transportation : Metro station Madeleine, RER Auber - Buses 24, 42, 43, 52, 84 and 94.*

The passageway gives on the place de la Madeleine but is sheltered from the traffic noise, therefore this hotel is quiet. It was renovated in Louis XIII style, this isn't shocking in the least for it goes well with the large proportions of all the rooms. The lobby is decorated with a tapestry, beams, stone walls, light-coloured floor tiles and Medieval furniture, it is also brightened by a light well. The corridors are dark red, on the walls were hung pictures showing the Flanders... The rooms are covered with flowered, rose or buff-coloured tapestries matching the curtains. The white lace bedspreads brighten up this decoration. Usually spacious, the rooms are cosy, those with two windows, whose number ends with 3 are the more agreeable. All the bathrooms are tiled white or beige, the tables set around the washbasins are of red marble. To your disposal, in each room, you will find a shoe brush and a sewing kit, isn't this a good idea ? Downstairs, for breakfast you will be served yogurts, corn flakes, creams and cakes. Here, the staff really looks after the comfort of its clientele.

Hôtel Favart ★★★

5 rue Marivaux - 75002 Paris
Tel. : (1) 42 97 59 83 - Telex : 213 126 - Fax : (1) 40 15 95 58
Manager : Mr Champetier

♦ *37 sound-proofed rooms (except on the 1st floor) with shower or bath, direct dial line, TV, "Alphapage" contact system and safe* ♦ *Independant Italian restaurant* ♦ *Prices : single : 460 F ; double : 550 F ; triple : 650 F - Extra bed : 75 F* ♦ *Breakfast : 20 F* ♦ *No off-season* ♦ *Credit cards : American Express and Visa* ♦ *Facilities : reservations, laundry, dry-cleaning* ♦ *Dogs allowed* ♦ *Parking facilities : place de la Bourse* ♦ *Transportation : Metro station Richelieu-Drouot, RER Auber - Buses 20, 21, 27, 29, 81 and 95.*

Goya lived here. Generations of Spaniards came after him, faithful to an atmosphere : the tradition of the Hôtel Favart goes back to the 18th century. The management still wishes to maintain a gracious welcome, an interior decoration which combines the luxury of space with a quiet atmosphere, and service carried out by a courteous staff, attached to this place for many years. The Opera Comique (light opera) is right opposite. The hotel has it's "ambiance" ; a vast lobby, punctuated by round and smooth beige marble columns and small red and black tub chairs between the desk of fine elm wood and the stairway decorated with scenes of Parisian life. The rooms have a very "French" 18th century or Louis-Philippe style decoration and dedicated to two colours : blue and beige. Here, colours make the difference... and what a difference ! You will then like the good size of the rooms, the silence, the convenient cupboard space and the comfort of the bathrooms, sometimes a little old-fashioned but often lighted by a window... Do we have to add that this is one of our favourites ?

Hôtel de Noailles ★★★

9 rue de la Michodière - 75002 Paris
Tel. : (1) 47 42 92 90 - Telex : 290 644 - Fax : (1) 49 24 92 71
Manager : Mrs Falck

♦ *58 sound-proofed rooms with bath, direct dial line and TV*
♦ *Patio, bar, conference room* ♦ *Prices : single : 560 F ; double :*
710 F ; triple : 810 F ♦ *Breakfast with orange juice : 35 F* ♦ *Off-*
season : 15 July to 31 August ♦ *Credit card : Visa* ♦ *Facilities :*
reservations, laundry, dry-cleaning, snacks ♦ *Dogs allowed*
♦ *Parking facilities : place de la Bourse and rue du Marché-Saint-*
Honoré ♦ *Transportation : Metro stations Opéra or 4-Septembre,*
RER Auber - Buses 20, 21, 27, 29, 39, 68, 81 and 95.

Lauren Bacall and Humphrey Bogart would feel at ease in this
completely new hotel, very contemporary but with a touch of
nostalgia, reminding imperceptibly of post-war thriller movies. A
vast entrance with beautiful marble flooring leads to the bar and the
living room (entirely black and white but extremely comfortable), in
a cloud of film-like light. In the back, a patio, arranged in a
Japanese way, diffuses its light onto the elegant ground floor
surprisingly calm in such an animated district. Bright-coloured
corridors (green, bright blue, grey or peacock blue, depending on
the floor), punctuated with large armchairs and a small welcoming
sitting room, lead to the rooms – all are identical – where the
decoration takes on the tones and tendancies of the ground floor.
Quite large, well lit, quiet, always comfortable, they all have
bathrooms with sparkling chrome, covered with marble or white
tiles.
A welcome full of youth and sweet breakfast-buffets add a cheerful
note to this very attractive hotel.

Hôtel Gaillon-Opéra ★★★

9 rue Gaillon - 75002 Paris
Tel. : (1) 47 42 47 74 - Telex : 215 716 - Fax : (1) 47 42 01 23
Manager : Mrs Wolecki

♦ *26 sound-proofed rooms with bath, direct dial line, TV, hair-drier, safe and minibar* ♦ *Prices : single : 600 F ; double : 700 F - Extra bed : 100 F* ♦ *Breakfast : 35 F* ♦ *No off-season* ♦ *Credit cards : American Express, Diners and Visa* ♦ *Facilities : reservations, laundry, dry-cleaning, snacks* ♦ *Dogs allowed* ♦ *Parking facilities : 58 rue du Marché-Saint-Honoré, place Vendôme and opposite 15 rue des Pyramides* ♦ *Transportation : Metro station Opéra or 4-Septembre, RER Auber - Buses 20, 21, 27, 29, 39, 68, 81 and 95.*

Never rely on appearances ! In this shopping and business area, this is a building among others. But it is also an attractive hotel, because once you are inside it has the charm of a country inn. Renovated in 1987 and 1988, priority was given to comfort. No revolutionary design, but beautiful material (marble and warm tints of wood), very cosy Louis-Philippe or rustic furniture, with big bunches of flowers. Everything is simple. Add to this a reception desk, situated between a patio and a bay window, where six languages are spoken – a record ! – and where good service is a priority.
The rooms are impeccable : they are papered in salmon pink or sky blue, with bedspreads made of patchwork ; they have beams on the first floor and sloping ceiling on the seventh, the lighting is soft. The rather small bathrooms, in beige or pink marble, are well thought out. Everywhere you'll find perfect silence. Nicely served in the lounge, breakfast is extremely good. Here, clearly, people like to please.

Hôtel de Castille ★★★★

37 rue Cambon - 75001 Paris
Tel. : (1) 42 61 55 20 - Telex : 213 505 - Fax : (1) 40 15 97 64
Manager : Mr Langlois

♦ *61 rooms and 15 duplex apt. with shower or bath, direct dial line, TV by satellite and video, (trouser-press in the duplex apt.)*
♦ *Patio, bar, restaurant (closed on Saturdays, Sundays and public holidays), conference room* ♦ *Prices : single : 1 190 F ; double : 1 450 F ; duplex apt. : 1 800 to 2 400 F - Extra bed : 200 F*
♦ *Breakfast : 60 F* ♦ *Off-season : winter (exclusive of professional shows), May and August* ♦ *Credit cards : Air+, American Express, Diners, En Route, JCB and Visa* ♦ *Facilities : reservations, laundry, dry-cleaning, snacks* ♦ *Dogs allowed*
♦ *Parking facilities : 39 rue Cambon, 7 rue Caumartin and place Vendôme* ♦ *Transportation : Metro station Madeleine, RER Auber - Buses 24, 42, 52, 84 and 94.*

Style and space are the main characteristics of this well organized 4-star, located between the place Vendôme and the Madeleine.
The very bright and vast hallway of polished marble ends with an extremely nice bar : dark-red velvet armchairs, low tables with the transparency of glass and beyond the picture window, a very pretty patio. In the large rooms (here lies the true luxury of this hotel), the lines are sharp, they are identical, beige or pale grey. Light wood for the furniture (inspired by the 1930s), lined in dark grey, hung with lithographs by Erté, lit by gilt brass lamps. The pretty white bathrooms, underlined with grey marble, are also spacious. Real duplex apartments with high ceilings, and on the sixth floor, on the street side, a glimpse of the colonne Vendôme and the trees of the Ministry of Justice. The facilities of a 4-star, large volumes, a nice area : all characteristics which make a good address.

Hôtel Family ★★

35 rue Cambon - 75001 Paris
Tel. : (1) 42 61 54 84
Manager : Mrs Steinbach

♦ *25 rooms and 1 suite with shower or bath, direct dial line and TV*
♦ *Prices : single : 375 F ; double : 510 F ; triple : 640 F ; suite :*
1 000 F - Extra bed : 130 F ♦ *Breakfast : 25 F* ♦ *Off-season :*
January and November ♦ *Credit cards : American Express and*
Visa ♦ *Facilities : reservations, laundry, dry-cleaning, snacks*
♦ *Dogs allowed* ♦ *Parking facilities : 7 rue Caumartin and place*
Vendôme ♦ *Transportation : Metro station Madeleine, RER*
Auber - Buses 24, 42, 52, 84 and 94.

Unexpected between the place Vendôme and the Faubourg Saint-Honoré, this very simple hotel, with only 2 stars, but much personality. The manager has just rearranged the lobby to add a small white lounge furnished with Chesterfield leather armchairs and decorated with a bouquet standing in front of a mirror. The corridors are painted white, the mouldings pink and in the basement you'll find a breakfast room. However, indifferent to the surrounding luxury, Mrs Steinbach just freshened up the off-white rooms furnished in a delicious pre-1940s style : sculpted dark wood, majestic cupboards with beveled mirrors and an assortment of dressing tables and chairs ; bathrooms enclosed in wooden folding screens with golden flower studs and small engraved glass. The larger rooms bear numbers in 1 or 2. On the fifth floor, a very, very nice apartment, big and classic. On the fourth and fifth floors, on the street side, you'll see the colonne Vendôme pointing through the chesnut trees of the Ministry of Finances.

Hôtel des Tuileries ★★★

10 rue Sainte-Hyacinthe - 75001 Paris
Tel. : (1) 42 61 04 17 - Telex : 240 744 - Fax : (1) 49 27 91 56
Manager : Mrs Poulle-Vidal

♦ *26 rooms (24 sound-proofed and air-conditioned), with bath, direct dial line, TV, hair-drier, trouser-press, safe and minibar* ♦ *Prices : single : 605 to 890 F ; double : 690 to 1 090 F ; triple : + 30%* ♦ *Breakfast with fresh fruit juice, cheese and fruit : 45 F* ♦ *Off-season : January and August* ♦ *Credit cards : American Express, Diners, Eurocard, MasterCard and Visa* ♦ *Facilities : reservations, laundry, dry-cleaning, snacks, catering for small parties* ♦ *Dogs allowed* ♦ *Parking facilities : place du Marché-Saint-Honoré* ♦ *Transportation : Metro stations Tuileries or Pyramides - Buses 21, 27, 68, 69 and 72.*

In this old town house built at the end of the 18th century and where it is said that Marie-Antoinette once stayed, one is welcomed with almost slavic warmth in a typically French decor with beautiful antique furniture, carpets, stylish furnishings and a light well which brightens up the lobby and staircase. This is the Inn of Silence : carpets over moquette in the corridors and the rooms which are isolated from the corridor by a little entrance, and as efficiently protected from the street noise by special windows. Equipped by a practical mind (large wardrobes, good lighting, useful extra furniture and a "dumb" electrical valet), these rooms are all the more agreeable that they are pretty : high-ceilinged on the second floor, lighted by half-moon windows on the first floor and always furnished with refinement (writing desk, chest of drawers, small table). The wallpaper adds a touch of originality, now modern, now damask, with flowers or of Japanese inspiration. And in the bathrooms (of beige marble), there is a corner washstand where it was necessary to save space. Obviously, in this slightly expensive hotel, nothing is left to chance, but it is such a pleasant place to stay.

Hôtel Duminy-Vendôme ★★★

3 rue du Mont-Thabor - 75001 Paris
Tel. : (1) 42 60 32 80 - Telex : 213 492 - Fax : (1) 42 96 07 83
Manager : Mr Clayeux

♦ *79 rooms with shower or bath, direct dial line, TV and minibar* ♦ *Bar* ♦ *Prices : single : 600 F ; double : 780 to 890 F - Extra bed : 120 F* ♦ *Breakfast included* ♦ *Credit cards : American Express, Diners, Eurocard, JCB, MasterCard and Visa* ♦ *Facilities : reservations, laundry, dry-cleaning* ♦ *No dogs allowed* ♦ *Parking facilities : place Vendôme and place du Marché-Saint-Honoré* ♦ *Transportation : Metro stations Concorde or Tuileries, RER Auber - Buses 21, 42, 52, 68 and 72.*

In a street unexpectedly calm for an area so close to the Tuileries, this hotel will surprise you in many ways. Nothing is left from the "Club des Feuillants" pulled down after the Revolution's Reign of Terror, but the 1925 furniture, which has an almost rustic charm without lacking a certain refined simplicity, this was preserved as much as possible when the house was renovated in 1984. High brass beds, bronze bracket lamps, writing desks, dressing tables, wardrobes, seats and marquetry : in the rooms, every piece of furniture is a period piece... or in a similar style, including the bluish wallpaper matching the curtains. Only the bathrooms are of beige marble.

The columns, the glass roof, the mirrors and the wooden lattice work give a different character to the lounge. A beautiful glass partition hides the cosy bar which boasts of an interesting wine list. In the back, a tiny garden adds a nostalgic note.

Seventy-nine rooms may be a lot, but each customer is treated with the same individual attention as in a "nice little family-owned hotel", except that here it is more expensive.

Hôtel de la Tamise ★★★

**4 rue d'Alger - 75001 Paris
Tel. : (1) 42 60 51 54 - Fax : (1) 42 86 89 97
Manager : Mrs Bellec**

♦ *20 rooms with washbasins, shower or bath ; phone : through the switchboard* ♦ *Prices : single : 170 to 530 F ; double : 370 to 530 F ; triple : 680 F* ♦ *Breakfast : 30 F* ♦ *Off-season : winter (exclusive of professional shows)* ♦ *Credit card : Visa* ♦ *Facilities : reservations* ♦ *Dogs allowed* ♦ *Parking facilities : place Vendôme and place du Marché-Saint-Honoré* ♦ *Transportation : Metro stations Tuileries or Concorde, RER Auber - Buses 68, 69 and 72.*

This discreet and somewhat old-fashioned hotel is located within a stone's throw from the Tuileries Gardens in a little street perpendicular to the rue de Rivoli.

On either side of the entrance hall are two small, pleasant lounges with beautiful English furniture. An old-fashioned lift goes up to the rooms, these are more or less large but always simple, with wallpaper showing little blue and pink flowers. The very classic bathrooms are decorated in the same shades.

Small but very respectable, this old and traditional hotel has two major assets : its location and very reasonable rates for this area.

Hôtel Brighton ★★★

218 rue de Rivoli - 75001 Paris
Tel. : (1) 42 60 30 03 - Telex : 217 431 - Fax : (1) 42 60 41 78
Manager : Mr Hashimoto

♦ *73 rooms with shower or bath, direct dial line, TV, safe and minibar* ♦ *Prices : single or double : 330 to 675 F ; suite : 900 F - Extra bed : 110 F* ♦ *Breakfast : 30 F* ♦ *Off-season : January, February and August* ♦ *Credit cards : American Express, Diners and Visa* ♦ *Facilities : reservations, laundry, dry-cleaning* ♦ *No dogs allowed* ♦ *Parking facilities : place Vendôme and place du Marché-Saint-Honoré* ♦ *Transportation : Metro stations Tuileries or Palais-Royal - Buses 21, 27, 29, 68, 72, 81 and 95.*

Overlooking the Tuileries Gardens, this hotel still retains a certain magic from the splendour of bygone days. Facing trees, the top floors offer one of the most beautiful views of Paris. Bedrooms are like ballrooms furnished in 19th century style : high ceilings with ornamental mouldings, wide windows, lush draperies, small round tables with marble tops, period chairs and armchairs and huge brass beds. Last of all, as if all this were only a prologue, the bathrooms are amazing : they are not big but immense, not beautiful but sublime. The one for room #115 shines from floor to ceiling with the gold of its mosaics.

About 30 rooms on the garden side display the same splendour as in the past. The rooms giving on the courtyard seem all the more ordinary. But they will definitely look better after the renovation which is going on, one floor at a time, over three years.

Hôtel Molière ★★★

21 rue Molière - 75001 Paris
Tel. : (1) 42 96 22 01 - Telex : 213 292 - Fax : (1) 42 60 48 68
Managers : Mr and Mrs Perraud

♦ *30 rooms and 3 suites, sound-proofed on the street side, with shower or bath, direct dial line, TV by satellite and video, hair-drier and minibar* ♦ *Prices : single : 370 to 530 F ; double : 470 to 580 F ; suite : 1 000 F - Extra bed : 100 F* ♦ *Breakfast with orange juice : 35 F ; buffet : 50 F* ♦ *No off-season* ♦ *Credit cards : American Express, Diners, Eurocard, MasterCard and Visa* ♦ *Facilities : reservations* ♦ *No dogs allowed* ♦ *Parking facilities : 58 rue du Marché-Saint-Honoré and opposite 15 rue des Pyramides* ♦ *Transportation : Metro stations Palais-Royal or Pyramides, RER Auber - Bus 20, 21, 27, 39, 68, 81 and 95.*

Cherubs and ironwork on the balconies give character to this 19th century façade. When it was renovated in 1989, Mr and Mrs Perraud took great care of this architecture and of the pre-war furniture. The decoration of padded walls, muted tones, lightened by bright-coloured prints on a dark background, creates a muffled atmosphere. In the hallway, round columns painted to look like marble ; in the back, the building's flowered courtyard… Upstairs, where the floor is covered by brown moquette, the rooms are furnished in two different styles : 1930s, with low brass beds, high night tables, small round armchairs, dressing table with reclining mirror ; or Louis XVI, with caned chairs and bedheads, light colour painted wood… They all have a nice size ; mauve, blue or yellow shades with coordinated prints, and when there is an alcove, it opens onto a closet or a nicely old-fashioned bathroom. A well-managed 3-star hotel.

Grand Hôtel de Champagne ★★★

13 rue des Orfèvres - 75001 Paris
Tel. : (1) 42 36 60 00 - Telex : 215 955 - Fax : (1) 45 08 43 33
Managers : Mr and Mrs Lauferon

♦ *40 rooms and 3 suites, sound-proofed, with shower or bath, direct dial line, cable TV and Canal+, safe* ♦ *Prices : single or double with shower or bath : 510 to 670 F ; suite : 940 to 1 000 F - Extra bed : 150 F* ♦ *Breakfast with fruit juice, eggs, corn flakes, cold meats, cheese and fresh fruit (buffet) : 50 F* ♦ *Off-season : 15 July to 31 August* ♦ *Credit cards : American Express, Diners and Visa* ♦ *Facilities : reservations, laundry, dry-cleaning* ♦ *Dogs allowed* ♦ *Parking facilities : Les Halles* ♦ *Transportation : Metro station Châtelet, RER Châtelet-Les-Halles - Buses 21, 38, 47, 58, 67, 69, 70, 72, 74, 75, 76, 81 and 85.*

The towers of the Conciergerie are on the other side of the Seine river, and the nearby rue de Rivoli marks the limit between the district (listed) of this old house and the Forum des Halles. This house used to be the hotel of tailors members of the Compagnons du Tour de France (a beam dated 1562 witnesses this past), and it still has nooks and crannies, beams and stones ; Mr and Mrs Lauferon, taken by the place's originality, imagined rooms that are all different.

Pink or sea green, Louis XIII or Louis XV style, funny and large like room #301 with its lacquer effects, two levels and a 1960s decoration, all are very nice to live in and their bathrooms are gay (small sandstone tiles enamelled pink which highlight the brown or beige marble), they are sometimes entirely open to the room in order to respect its proportions. Our favourites are on the top floor, the attic with a large flowered balcony, where it must be nice to eat breakfast in the summer, except if you can't resist the buffet served downstairs : a true meal the house is proud of.

Hôtel Ducs d'Anjou ★★

1 rue Sainte-Opportune - 75001 Paris
Tel. : (1) 42 36 92 24 - Telex : 218 681 - Fax : (1) 42 36 16 63
Managers : Mr and Mrs Albar

♦ *38 sound-proofed rooms with shower or bath, direct dial line, cable TV and hair-drier* ♦ *Prices : single with shower or bath : 492 F ; double with shower or bath : 524 F ; triple or quadruple : 780 F - Extra bed : 50 F* ♦ *Breakfast with orange juice and cheese : 38 F* ♦ *Off-season : 15 July to 31 August* ♦ *Credit cards : American Express, Diners, En Route, JCB and Visa* ♦ *Facilities : reservations, laundry, dry-cleaning* ♦ *Dogs allowed* ♦ *Parking facilities : Les Halles* ♦ *Transportation : Metro station Châtelet, RER Châtelet-Les-Halles - Buses 21, 29, 38, 39, 47, 58, 67, 69, 70, 72, 74, 75, 76 and 81.*

In a very youthful district, chosen by some, disparaged by others (the hotel is within a stone's throw from the Forum des Halles), this place has been renovated only two years ago, adopting an airy and modern style. Both the dominant grey and the light give a feeling of space unusual in a hotel of this category. Even in the very agreeable vaulted basement. And from the entrance to the rooms, surfaces painted with pure colours brighten up the whole : hard blue leather sofas, a mat-red panel, brilliant prints flecked with black for the fabrics in the sober rooms, always tidy and practical. The view is very Parisian, out of the large fanlights of rooms #61 and #62 you'll see the tubular hight of Beaubourg, the lace of the tour Saint-Jacques and the zinc rooftops.

Quiet in the winter, the place Sainte-Opportune, on which half of the rooms give, becomes quite noisy in the summer. Our advice : stay on the last floors and on the other side where you'll take better advantage of the hotel's pretty semi-circle structure crowned by a balcony and neighbouring terraces.

Hôtel Britannique ★★★

20 avenue Victoria - 75001 Paris
Tel. : (1) 42 33 74 59 - Telex : 230 600 - Fax : (1) 42 33 82 65
Manager : Mr Danjou

♦ *40 sound-proofed rooms with shower or bath, direct dial line, TV by satellite, hair-drier and minibar* ♦ *Prices : single : 470 F ; double : 570 to 650 F - Extra bed : 70 F* ♦ *Breakfast with fruit juice, corn flakes and eggs : 40 F* ♦ *Off-season : 15 July to 31 August* ♦ *Credit cards : American Express, Diners and Visa* ♦ *Facilities : reservations* ♦ *No dogs allowed* ♦ *Parking facilities : Hôtel-de-Ville and quai de Gesvres* ♦ *Transportation : Metro station Châtelet, RER Châtelet-Les-Halles - Buses 21, 38, 47, 58, 67, 69, 70, 72, 74, 75, 76, 81 and 85.*

The avenue Victoria has the charm of those streets where you feel that you are breathing country air. Plane trees, flower vendors, shops for gardening ware have invaded this short avenue which is separated from the banks of the Seine river, with its booksellers, seed shops and bird sellers, by the Théâtre du Châtelet. This hotel was built by the British at the time when the avenue was being opened ; it was held by the same family until 1978. Renovation did not take away its welcoming atmosphere : here, people smile, listen to you and spend as much time as needed to get you accustomed to the place. It is arranged in such a way that it is pleasant to look at, without ever sacrificing comfort to decoration. Large beige flooring with black studs and varnished wood for the lobby. Dark-red lacquered woodworks underline the grey walls of the lounge below, with large leather armchairs and sofas. Dark-blue moquette edged with soft-pink leaves runs along the staircase and the corridors. The rooms, where pastel shades predominate, are all of a good size, carefully lit and sound-proofed ; the bathrooms are well equipped. This hotel is a most pleasant place to stay.

Hôtel Louvre - Forum ★★★

25 rue du Bouloi - 75001 Paris
Tel. : (1) 42 36 54 19 - Telex : 240 288 - Fax : (1) 42 33 66 31
Manager : Mrs Prin

◆ *28 rooms with shower or bath, direct dial line, TV and minibar*
◆ *Prices : single : 360 F ; double : 410 to 450 F - Extra bed :*
100 F ◆ *Breakfast : 28 F* ◆ *Off-season : December and August*
◆ *Credit cards : American Express, Diners and Visa* ◆ *Facilities :*
reservations, laundry, dry-cleaning ◆ *Dogs allowed* ◆ *Parking*
facilities : 10 rue Bailleul ◆ *Transportation : Metro stations*
Louvre or Palais-Royal, RER Châtelet-Les-Halles - Buses 29, 48,
67, 74 and 85.

Located halfway between the Palais Royal and Les Halles, in a quiet
little street of this animated neighbourhood, this hotel has a pretty
façade with white shutters along each of its six storeys. Inside, two
places are worth noting : first, the lobby, which is most attractive
with its wooden beams, its tiled flooring with large sandstone slabs
on which carpets add a touch of warmth, and its sitting room corner
furnished in Louis XV style and brightened by a mirror and a big
bouquet ; second, comes the basement where breakfast is served in a
very pleasant room furnished in Louis XIII style with beautiful gilt
mirrors. Upstairs ? All is new, even the corridors covered with blue,
green or pink woolen tiny-striped fabric and pretty flowered cotton
fabric and still the superb doors, made of gnarled elm wood. In the
rooms, there is steel or cane furniture. The rooms on the top floor,
with their sloping ceiling are the nicest. The bathrooms are usually
big and a bit old-fashioned. How is it then that one feels so
comfortable in this hotel, which is on the whole somewhat modest
for its 3 stars ? The spontaneity of the welcome, an always helpful
attitude and reasonnable prices no doubt play an important role.

Hôtel Agora ★★

7 rue de la Cossonnerie - 75001 Paris
Tel. : (1) 42 33 46 02 - Fax : (1) 42 33 80 99
Manager : Mr de Marco

♦ *29 sound-proofed rooms with shower or bath, direct dial line and* TV ♦ *No breakfast room* ♦ *Prices : single : 330 to 530 F ; double : 350 to 550 F - Extra bed : 100 F* ♦ *Breakfast : 30 F* ♦ *Off-season : July and August* ♦ *Credit cards : American Express, and Visa* ♦ *Facilities : reservations* ♦ *No dogs allowed* ♦ *Parking facilities : Les Halles* ♦ *Transportation : Metro stations Les Halles or Châtelet, RER Châtelet-Les-Halles - Buses 21, 29, 38, 39, 47, 58, 67, 69, 70, 72, 74, 75, 76 and 81.*

The unusual façade of this small building may have inspired the interior decoration of this hotel : a stairway hung with grey fabric leads to the lobby on the first floor, where reigns an organized bric-à-brac. On the black and white tiled floor, you will find 19th century furniture, wooden statuettes, green plants everywhere ; underneath the paper frieze hang green and white flowered drapes, on the walls we see engravings of Andromaque next to Moses and Wagner. A microscopic lift goes up to rooms papered in green, pink, blue or pale yellow, depending on the floor (the bathrooms are in matching colours). Here, the decoration is less disorderly. 19th century furniture, pretty chests of drawers, mirrors, a plant in an antique pot, an old lamp and sometimes a marble mantelpiece over the fireplace impart to each room its private character. The corner rooms with two windows are big and light ; those whose number ends with 1 have a small entrance hall and on the sixth floor the ceilings slope down to the floor. In this animated district of the Forum des Halles, this is an amusing, youthful and very Italian-like hotel. Perfect in winter when no one would think of opening the windows.

Hôtel Saint-Merry ★★★

78 rue de la Verrerie - 75004 Paris
Tel. : (1) 42 78 14 15 - Fax : (1) 40 29 06 82
Manager : Mr Crabbe

♦ *12 rooms with shower or bath, direct dial line* ♦ *No lift or breakfast room* ♦ *Prices : single or double with shower (no WC) : 380 and 400 F, with shower : 630 F, with bath : 800 F ; triple : 800 and 900 F* ♦ *Breakfast : 40 F* ♦ *Off-season : January and August* ♦ *No credit cards accepted* ♦ *Facilities : reservations, laundry* ♦ *Dogs allowed* ♦ *Parking facilities : place Georges-Pompidou and Hôtel-de-Ville* ♦ *Transportation : Metro stations Hôtel-de-Ville or Châtelet, RER Châtelet-Les-Halles - Buses 58, 70, 72, 74 and 76.*

This is probably the only hotel in Paris where a flying buttress goes right through a room (#9). It is owned by the church Saint-Merri, the hotel being in fact the former presbitary.

It is terribly gothic or rather, neo-gothic. There is the folding closet-bed for the night watchman or the phone booth in the lobby. An auction room frequenter, Mr Crabbe brings back from his rounds decorated woodwork and furniture which give a personal character to the smallest nook or cranny. Chairs, tables, bedheads, wardrobes, all of this is gothic, with a beautiful patina and carefully waxed (however, the bathrooms are functional, more classic, and tiled in little mosaics matching the colour of the adjoining room). Bayadere bedspreads of a dull rose or soft green go well with the decoration as a whole. No television, the management hates them.

Within a stone's throw from Beaubourg, this curiosity is also a good and very welcoming hotel.

Hôtel Beaubourg ★★★

11 rue Simon-Lefranc - 75004 Paris
Tel. : (1) 42 74 34 24 - Telex : 216 100
Manager : Mr and Mrs Morand

♦ *28 sound-proofed rooms with shower or bath, TV, hair-drier and minibar, direct dial line* ♦ *Prices : single or double with shower : 430 F, with bath : 490 to 540 F - Extra bed : 150 F* ♦ *Breakfast : 30 F* ♦ *Off-season : August* ♦ *Credit cards : American Express, Diners and Visa* ♦ *Facilities : reservations, laundry, dry-cleaning* ♦ *No dogs allowed* ♦ *Parking facilities : Beaubourg* ♦ *Transportation : Metro stations Hôtel-de-Ville or Rambuteau, RER Châtelet-Les-Halles - Buses 29, 38, 47, 58, 67, 69, 70, 72, 74, 75 and 76.*

Mr and Mrs Morand made a very agreeable and quiet 3-star hotel – 100 yards away from Beaubourg – out of a building in a pretty bad state only three years ago. A godsend for people attracted to the Centre Pompidou and the art galleries around. Intimate atmosphere, walls lined with ginger-coloured buckskin, leather sofas, oriental rugs, wainscotting and exposed beams in the lobby.

A little flowered lawn and a terrace with tiny white pebbles (unfortunately inaccessible) give light to the corridors and the rooms on the courtyard side (the majority). The bigger rooms, on the street side, are decorated with pretty flowered fabrics, brown wood furniture and marble tiled bathrooms. On the other side, they chose brass beds, painted wood, flowered fabrics and still very good bathrooms. If you like to have breakfast in fresh air, ask for room #4 on the ground floor : it has a terrace. If you like originality, large bathrooms and sloping ceilings, ask for room #51.

Impeccable, comfortable, quiet and with reasonnable rates, this could be an excellent address. Too bad the breakfast lacks originality and the managers are amiable but nothing more.

Hôtel de la Bretonnerie ★★★

**22 rue Sainte-Croix-de-la-Bretonnerie - 75004 Paris
Tel. : (1) 48 87 77 63 - Fax : (1) 42 77 26 78
Managers : Mr and Mrs Sagot**

♦ *Closed from 20 July to 20 August* ♦ *31 rooms, sound-proofed on the street side, with shower or bath, direct dial line and* TV ♦ *Prices : single : 380 to 700 F ; double : 500 to 700 F ; suite : 800 F - Extra bed : 120 F* ♦ *Breakfast : 38 F* ♦ *Credit cards : Eurocard, MasterCard and Visa* ♦ *Facilities : reservations, laundry, dry-cleaning* ♦ *Small dogs allowed* ♦ *Parking facilities : garage nearby and Hôtel-de-Ville* ♦ *Transportation : Metro station Hôtel-de-Ville - Buses 29, 38, 47, 58, 67, 69, 70, 72, 74, 75 and 76.*

Do not judge this hotel on its entrance hall : it is not up to the standard of the rest of the hotel, recently renovated with taste and skill. The main quality of the rooms is space, then comes the care with which they were decorated. The high ceilings made it possible to build several mezzanines, confering on these rooms similar advantages to those of suites. Honey-coloured tints predominate – beams, moquettes, Louis XIII or Louis-Philippe furniture – illuminated by the bright-white door frames and bedspreads. The lighting is well distributed. The bathrooms of beige marble or rustic brown tiles are carefully finished and match, from the tiled floor to the ceiling, the fabrics in the rooms. The third floor rooms have lower ceilings but are still spacious ; some of them have a window in their bathroom ; on the fourth floor, under the roof, an exception : the peonies of the wallpaper between the beams. We particularly liked the apartment overlooking the backyard : romantic, fresh, luminous, it is composed of two rooms, pink and white, with cretonne print and fine net curtains...
In the basement, a vaulted room where breakfast is served becomes a lounge-bar in the afternoon.

Hôtel du 7e Art ★★

20 rue Saint-Paul - 75004 Paris
Tel. : (1) 42 77 04 03 - Fax : (1) 42 77 69 10
Manager : Mr Kenig

♦ *23 rooms with shower or bath, direct dial line and cable* TV
♦ *Restaurant, conference room* ♦ *Prices : single or double 360 to 410 F ; junior-suite : 480 and 550 F - Extra bed : 100 F* ♦ *Breakfast with orange juice : 30 F* ♦ *Credit cards : American Express, Diners and Visa* ♦ *Facilities : reservations* ♦ *Dogs allowed* ♦ *Parking facilities : 2 rue Geoffroy-l'Asnier and 16 rue Saint-Antoine* ♦ *Transportation : Metro stations Saint-Paul or Pont-Marie - Buses 67, 69, 76 and 96.*

Located in a more secret part of the Marais, close to the Seine river, this friendly hotel has taken the motion pictures as theme for its decoration : from its visiting card to the checkered carpeting in the stairway, everything here is black and white. It is fun and well done. The rooms (most of them not big) are pebble-dashed, with heavy cream-coloured cotton curtains, light-coloured wood furniture, a dark moquette and on the wall always hangs a photo or a poster of a motion picture classic. The third floor is very luminous and the twin bedded rooms are quite big. On the fourth floor, two suites with sloping ceilings and a double exposure are very agreeable, and can lodge four people behind their short, sashed curtains. The bathrooms are impeccably white except for the black and white floor tiles ; they are small but well equipped. At the bar-restaurant the hotel guests can mingle with antique dealers from the nearby "village Saint-Paul". In winter, you should find a blazing log fire in the sitting room corner of the restaurant furnished with armchairs, bistro chairs and tables, black of course, while walls are light-coloured. This is a lively and friendly place, with moderate rates and in a nice area, what more can one ask ?

Hôtel des Célestins ★★

1 rue Charles-V - 75004 Paris
Tel. : (1) 48 87 87 04
Managers : Mr and Mrs Record

♦ *15 rooms with shower or bath, direct dial line* ♦ *No lift*
♦ *Prices : single : 370 F ; double with shower : 400 F, with bath :*
510 F ; triple with bath : 650 F ♦ *Breakfast : 30 F* ♦ *Off-season :*
February and November ♦ *Credit card : Visa* ♦ *Facilities :*
reservations, laundry ♦ *Small dogs allowed* ♦ *Parking facilities :*
16 rue Saint-Antoine ♦ *Transportation : Metro stations Saint-Paul*
or Bastille - Buses 67, 69, 76 and 96.

With one foot in the Marais, the other at the Bastille, in a quiet old
street near the riverbanks and the Ile Saint-Louis, this hotel is a
17th century building which used to be an annex of the Celestins
convent.
From the street one can see, through the little window panes, a
lobby decorated in Louis XIII style. The existing materials – stone
and wood – were used to good advantage. There, comfortable
armchairs were set.
Beautiful, gently sloping stairs, listed as historical monument, lead
to rooms decorated in the same spirit : rustic and cosy. The walls are
covered with greyish green or striped cotton fabric, cream-coloured
quilts cover the beds and Genovese velvet curtains hang from the
windows. The bathrooms are particularly pretty : tubs, washstands
and tiles are in baked lava enamelled in ultramarine blue, pink or
yellow. A small, welcoming hotel in the centre of what gives Paris
its charm.

Grand Hôtel Jeanne d'Arc ★★

3 rue de Jarente - 75004 Paris
Tel. : (1) 48 87 62 11
Managers : Mr and Mrs Aymard

♦ *37 rooms with shower or bath, direct dial line and cable TV*
♦ *Prices : single : 250 F ; double : 300 F ; triple : 360 F*
♦ *Breakfast : 27 F* ♦ *No off-season* ♦ *Credit card : Visa*
♦ *Facilities : reservations, laundry, dry-cleaning* ♦ *No dogs allowed*
♦ *Parking facilities : 16 rue Saint-Antoine* ♦ *Transportation :*
Metro station Saint-Paul - Buses 29, 67, 69, 76 and 96.

This hotel may be modest but it is unusual. This is mostly due to Mrs Aymard, a woman with a strong personality, who, when she has a free minute sits behind the reception desk and crochets superb white doilies which little by little have invaded all the ground floor. Greenery, small quilted seats that are amusing or frankly rustic as in the adjoining dining room, flowered carpets, window drapes with pompoms or flowers and a Christmas tree with flickering lights when it is the season, all these elements make this decoration like no other.

In total contrast with the baroque ground floor, the bedrooms are large, very large even, and perfectly straight lined. Extremely clean and renovated in blue or brick colours with a matching bathroom, those renovated last are pink. The sixth floor is the nicest.

If you don't count the service, a little insufficient, don't forget this is only a 2-star establishment, this hotel is amusing because of its undeniable character, its low prices and excellent location.

Hôtel Bastille-Spéria ★★★

1 rue de la Bastille - 75004 Paris
Tel. : (1) 42 72 04 01 - Telex : 214 327 - Fax : (1) 42 72 56 38
Managers : Mr and Mrs Clout

♦ *42 sound-proofed rooms with shower or bath, direct dial line, TV by satellite and Canal+, hair-drier and minibar* ♦ *Bar* ♦ *Prices : single with shower : 430 F, with bath : 460 F ; double with shower : 460 F, with bath : 520 F* ♦ *Breakfast with orange juice : 35 F* ♦ *Off-season : 15 July to 15 August and December until Christmas* ♦ *Credit cards : American Express, Diners and Visa* ♦ *Facilities : reservations* ♦ *Small dogs allowed* ♦ *Transportation : Metro station Bastille, RER Gare-de-Lyon - Buses 20, 29, 65, 69, 76, 86, 87 and 91.*

As we had expected, the Bastille Opera house and the recent "colonisation" of this area by artists and galleries gave a new look to hotels in this area.

Pretty and new (two years only) this hotel took on the neat and smooth appearance of the nearby Opera, with sharp lines and a very restful dominant grey colour in the two living room corners with leather sofas and in the adjoining dining room. A big aquarium, several rugs and a lot of greenery give life to the space of the ground floor.

Grey wooden furniture in the rooms, always agreeable ; we appreciate their exposed beams on the top floor, even in the bathrooms – pretty – with big rectangular washbasins.

Be careful, the facilities aren't special, but the price is reasonnable and the welcome is nice.

Hôtel Saint-Paul - Le Marais ★★★

8 rue de Sévigné - 75004 Paris
Tel. : (1) 48 04 97 27 - Telex : 260 808 - Fax : (1) 48 87 37 04
Managers : Mrs Leguide and Marcovici

♦ *27 sound-proofed rooms with bath, direct dial line, TV and hair-drier* ♦ *Flowered courtyard, bar* ♦ *Prices : single : 470 F ; double : 550 and 570 F ; suite : 750 F - Extra bed : 100 F* ♦ *Breakfast with fruit juice, cheese and fresh fruit : 35 F* ♦ *Off-season : August* ♦ *Credit cards : American Express, Diners and Visa* ♦ *Facilities : reservations, laundry, dry-cleaning* ♦ *Small dogs allowed* ♦ *Parking facilities : 2 rue Geoffroy-l'Asnier and 16 rue Saint-Antoine* ♦ *Transportation : Metro station Saint-Paul - Buses 29, 67, 69, 76 and 96.*

Right in the centre of the Marais, this hotel is refreshing because it bears a contemporary spirit quite unusual in a district bound to Louis XIII style… The place des Vosges is within a stone's throw and the Bastille ten minutes away. In this house, only the exposed beams were kept from centuries past, and the pillars which sand colour is the tone of the hotel. The nice, light space of the ground floor is punctuated by black armchairs, plants and wallcoverings. Breakfast is served in the arched basement. The rooms were carefully renovated and sound-proofed (the rue de Sévigné is busy, choose the rooms overlooking the flowered courtyard, on the side of the rue d'Ormesson) and well arranged. Pretty contrasts between the dark lines of the exposed beams and the pastel shades monochrome of the walls, bedspreads and modern furniture ; the moquette is pink, blue or almond green ; white net curtains mask the windows. Immaculate bathrooms, tiled with faience, and mosaïcs on the floor. Add a smiling welcome : here is a hotel of quality where one would easily spend some time…

Hôtel des Chevaliers ★★★

30 rue de Turenne - 75003 Paris
Tel. : (1) 42 72 73 47 - Telex : 211 554 - Fax : (1) 42 72 54 10
Manager : Mrs Truffaut

♦ *24 sound-proofed rooms with bath, direct dial line, TV, hair-drier and safe ♦ Prices : single or double : 480 F - Extra bed : 150 F ♦ Breakfast with orange juice : 30 F ♦ Off-season : January and August ♦ Credit cards : American Express, Diners, Eurocard, MasterCard and Visa ♦ Facilities : reservations, laundry, dry-cleaning, snacks ♦ Dogs allowed ♦ Parking facilities : 16 rue Saint-Antoine ♦ Transportation : Metro stations Chemin-Vert, Saint-Paul or Bastille - Buses 20, 29, 65 and 96.*

Once again this is a very old building, as old as the place des Vosges. When it was renovated, some coins of that time were found in the basement.

Louis XIII style has appropriately been kept for the ground floor, the vaulted basement and the old abandonned well ; this hotel has maintained its pretty proportions with its olden beams and stones exposed. The rooms, in beige tinted pink shades are furnished with light wood, pertaining a soft and luminous air. If you have the choice, take a room with twin beds, they are bigger, or a room on the fourth or fifth floor with slightly sloping ceilings.

The location, the cheerful welcome and the prices, going up at a very slow pace. This is indeed a very good hotel.

Pavillon de la Reine ★★★★

28 place des Vosges - 75003 Paris
Tel. : (1) 42 77 96 40 - Telex : 216 160 - Fax : (1) 42 77 63 06
Manager : Mr Sudre

◆ *30 rooms and 23 apartments, sound-proofed and air-conditioned, with bath, direct dial line, TV by satellite, hair-drier and minibar* ◆ *Prices : single : 1 080 F ; double : 1 080 to 1 200 F ; triple : 1 700 F ; apartment : 1 700 to 2 500 F* ◆ *Breakfast with orange juice : 70 F* ◆ *Credit cards : American Express, Diners and Visa* ◆ *Facilities : reservations, laundry, dry-cleaning* ◆ *Dogs allowed* ◆ *Parking facilities : 25 spaces in the hotel* ◆ *Transportation : Metro stations Bastille and Saint-Paul - Buses 20, 29, 65, 69 and 96.*

Who has never dreamt one day of living place des Vosges ? This hotel now makes it possible, or almost. If the front porch is under the arcades of the square, the Pavillon itself is a modern copy in the style of the square's architecture and is placed at the back of a courtyard. However, it is a complete success. The simplicity of the façade of white stones and of the yard paved in the traditional way, with a lawn and some boxtrees contrasts with the tasteful opulence of the lobby : Louis XIII style, light-coloured walls and flooring, brown beams and curtains ; a rigour alleviated by glass partitions, mirrors and the big 18th century russet-coloured velvet sofa.

Separated from the corridor by an entrance hall, the rooms are comfortable and pretty, papered in brown ochre or blue ; decorated in the Spanish style with wooden and painted beds and cotton coverlets ; a genuine antique piece of furniture in each room enhances the decoration. The bathrooms are of a good size, tiled in beige marble. This hotel is definitly of the same type as the Relais Christine as regards the welcome, the style, and even the way breakfast is served...

Hôtel Quatre Saisons - Bastille ★★★

67 rue de Lyon - 75012 Paris
Tel. : (1) 40 01 07 17 - Fax : (1) 40 01 07 27
Manager : Mr Jallerat

♦ *30 rooms and 6 junior-suites, sound-proofed and air-conditioned, with bath, 2 direct dial lines, TV by satellite, hair-drier, safe and minibar* ♦ *Bar* ♦ *Prices : single or double : 900 F ; suite : 1 200 F* ♦ *Breakfast with orange juice : 40 F* ♦ *Off-season : 15 July to 15 August* ♦ *Facilities : reservations, laundry, dry-cleaning* ♦ *Transportation : Metro station Bastille, RER Gare-de-Lyon - Buses 20, 29, 65, 69, 76, 86, 87 and 91.*

A very fashionable little sign indicates this hotel in bright blue letters, the last one to have open (in July 1990) in this area.

Façade definitely modern – but it is only normal for this hotel facing the Opera – with a few steps leading to a light, cocoon-like and grey universe, from the basement to the attic, all very elegant.

A long sophisticated lobby – where luminous partitions with openwork design allow to glimpse at the bar and dining room – goes through the hotel to reach the street on the other side.

A feeling of peacefulness in the rooms where a harmony of grey with touches of pink could seem a bit austere to some. But we like their graphic decoration, the beautiful moquette, the writing case set in the thick partition wall, the mirroring panels and the wardrobes : perfect. Beautiful bathrooms with tiny grey tiles and with pretty little things to welcome you.

Choose the rooms giving on the rue Biscornet, more quiet in the summer.

A very successful 3-star, but the bill is quite expensive.

Hôtel Belle Epoque ★★★

66 rue de Charenton - 75012 Paris
Tel. : (1) 43 44 06 66 - Telex : 211 551 - Fax : (1) 43 44 10 25
Manager : Mrs Garboua

♦ *26 rooms and 3 suites, sound-proofed, with bath, direct dial line, TV and minibar* ♦ *Small patio, bar, restaurant, 3 conference rooms* ♦ *Prices : single : 500 F ; double : 650 F ; triple : 750 F ; suite : 900 F - Extra bed : 150 F* ♦ *Breakfast (buffet) : 45 F* ♦ *Off-season : December and January (except during the New Year period)* ♦ *Credit cards : American Express, Diners, JCB and Visa* ♦ *Facilities : reservations, laundry, dry-cleaning, snacks* ♦ *Small dogs allowed* ♦ *Parking facilities : Bastille* ♦ *Transportation : Metro station Ledru-Rollin, RER Gare-de-Lyon - Buses 20, 29, 61 and 86.*

A lot of pleasure and sense of humour inspired Mrs Garboua when she renovated this hotel which is, over its five floors, a true pastiche of a decor from the beginning of this century.
1920s hall with "elephant armchairs", leading to a small patio overloaded with greenery and flowers. The rooms are all spacious and jauntily withstand an assertive decoration, inspired by Ruhlmann or Printz (in particular #1922 and 1927 with private terraces) ; otherwise the rooms suggest in a more discreet fashion the style of that time : drawings, posters, wall lamps, furniture with neat lines and precious wood, everything is comfortable. Excellent bathrooms very up-to-date covered with grey or beige marble and energy-giving breakfast-buffets.
A hotel where spirit shows everywhere even in the names of the conference rooms : Sarah Bernhardt, Rudolf Valentino, Mistinguett.

Résidence du Pré ★★

15 rue Pierre-Sémard - 75009 Paris
Tel. : (1) 48 78 26 72 - Telex : 660 549
Managers : Mr and Mrs Dupré

♦ *40 sound-proofed rooms with shower or bath, direct dial line and TV* ♦ *Bar* ♦ *Prices : single : 365 F ; double : 395 to 410 F ; triple : 540 F* ♦ *Breakfast : 25 F* ♦ *Off-season : January, February and March* ♦ *Credit cards : American Express and Visa* ♦ *Facilities : reservations, laundry, dry-cleaning* ♦ *Dogs allowed* ♦ *Parking facilities : square Montholon and 7 rue Bleue* ♦ *Transportation : Metro station Poissonnière - Buses 26, 42, 43, 48, 49 and 85.*

Newly redone, decorated in pastel shades pertaining a feminine touch to sharp lines, the atmosphere reigning in this hotel is exceptionaly young and light. The salmon-pink lounge-bar is furnished with sea-green sofas and lead-white oak pieces ; the large bay windows give on an always peaceful street. The grey rooms are nice and comfortable, each has its colour used for everything from the quilted bedspreads to the light and practical painted furniture. Half of them give on a small courtyard also painted in salmon pink, brightened up in the summer by geraniums. The bathrooms are grey or beige but unfortunately, the majority only has a shower.
2-star rates for a 3-star quality. This is a good hotel.

Hôtel d'Albret ★★★

16 rue Pierre-Sémard - 75009 Paris
Tel. : (1) 42 85 19 59 - Telex : 281 843 - Fax : (1) 48 74 88 31
Manager : Mrs Nunes

◆ *34 sound-proofed rooms with bath, direct dial line, TV and safe*
◆ *Prices : single : 550 F ; double : 600 F - Extra bed : 75 F*
◆ *Breakfast : 25 F* ◆ *Credit cards : American Express, Diners and Visa* ◆ *Facilities : reservations, laundry, dry-cleaning* ◆ *Dogs allowed* ◆ *Parking facilities : square Montholon and 7 rue Bleue*
◆ *Transportation : Metro stations Poissonnière or Cadet - Buses 26, 32, 42, 43, 48, 49 and 85.*

The heavily ornamented façade of this house built in the middle of last century does not let you foresee the pure lines awaiting you in the entrance hall of this hotel, decorated in a 1930s style.
Wide rounded bays link the lobby to the lounge-bar decorated in nuances of grey, off-white and light beige from the flooring to the simple ornamental mouldings of the ceiling, and lighted by bracket lamps shaped like cupolas. Mirrors, art deco or Louis XVI style armchairs create a peaceful and refined atmosphere. Just as light but more simple, the breakfast room is comfortable.
Cotton fabrics showing small beige and reddish brown (or green) patterns flecked black, modern light oak furniture and glass bracket lamps decorate the rooms. The best ones are those bearing numbers in 1. In the bathrooms, the tiles are grey (our favorites), sandy-coloured or pink. A certain style, a careful welcome make this a good hotel.

Hôtel du Léman ★★★

20 rue de Trévise - 75009 Paris
Tel. : (1) 42 46 50 66 - Telex : 281 086 - Fax : (1) 48 24 27 59
Manager : Mrs Legrand

♦ *24 rooms, sound-proofed on street side, with bath, direct dial line, TV and video, hair-drier and minibar* ♦ *Prices : single : 520 F ; double : 640 F - Extra bed : 150 F* ♦ *Breakfast (brunch) : 30 F* ♦ *Off-season : December, January, July and August* ♦ *Credit cards : American Express, Diners, Eurocard, MasterCard and Visa* ♦ *Facilities : reservations, laundry, dry-cleaning, snacks* ♦ *Dogs allowed* ♦ *Parking facilities : 7 rue Bleue* ♦ *Transportation : Metro station Cadet - Buses 20, 26, 42, 48, 67, 74 and 85.*

In a district and a street where there are so many hotels, the transparent and neat modern entrance augurs well of this hotel which turns out being excellent. The white lobby is attractive, arranged without any set up idea it is a real pleasure to look at. An Italian altar gate in marble marquetry with openwork design panels the reception desk where a tiny Oriental divinity watches over the lobby. Beautiful rugs add a touch of warmth to the light-coloured flooring of the sitting room corner furnished with Régence style armchairs. In the basement, extraordinary brunches are served on round tables of polished granite, surrounded by straw-bottomed armchairs : cereal, eggs, cold meats, cheese, milk products, fresh fruit salad, dried fruit ! The rooms aren't large but they are light, the lighting is subtle, furnishing modern and clever. To give them some character there is a small 1930s armchair, a lithography, a corner with sloping ceiling or beams.

We recommend room #66 on the top floor with its sloping ceiling, it is luminous and the proportions are good. We also liked the 5 rooms whose number ends with 6, they are larger.

Hôtel de la Tour d'Auvergne ★★★

10 rue de La Tour-d'Auvergne - 75009 Paris
Tel. : (1) 48 78 61 60 - Telex : 281 604 - Fax : (1) 49 95 99 00
Manager : Mr Duval

♦ *25 sound-proofed rooms with bath, direct dial line, TV*
♦ *Prices : single : 500 F ; double : 660 F - Extra bed : 100 F*
♦ *Breakfast with orange juice : 30 F* ♦ *Off-season : November to March* ♦ *Credit cards : American Express, Diners and Visa*
♦ *Facilities : reservations, laundry, dry-cleaning, secretarial work*
♦ *No dogs allowed* ♦ *Parking facilities : square d'Anvers*
♦ *Transportation : Metro stations Cadet or Anvers - Buses 42, 43, 49 and 85.*

Slightly beneath the Butte Montmartre, the 9th arrondissement is a district with much character. The Hôtel de la Tour d'Auvergne is like that too. Not many places show such an accumulation of colours, materials and different styles without becoming unpleasant. But here the result is natural and delicious. The entrance welcomes you softly : marble flooring and pinkish walls. Then you walk to a small bar-lounge limited by columns drawn in trompe-l'œil, it livens up with the coming and going of regular clients who more or less know each other, and like to chat with Mrs Duval.

In the rooms, free rein is given to imagination ! Decorations Louis XV, Louis XVI, 1900s or art deco... Fabrics are plain, colourfully striped or flowered. Yellow, dark-blue, red, pastel shades... Many canopies and draperies at bedheads. It is very comfortable, the bathrooms are white and very clean. Add a touch of classicism in the breakfast room and the small conference room in the basement. A hotel with much charm. And so full of life !

Hôtel de Navarin and d'Angleterre ★★

8 rue de Navarin - 75009 Paris
Tel. : (1) 48 78 31 80 - Fax : (1) 48 74 14 09
Managers : Mr and Mrs Maylin

♦ *27 rooms with washbasins, shower or bath, direct dial line, (TV in large rooms)* ♦ *Garden ; no lift* ♦ *Prices : single or double with washbasins : 200 F, with shower or bath : 280 F* ♦ *Breakfast : 22 F* ♦ *Credit card : Visa* ♦ *Facilities : reservations, laundry, dry-cleaning* ♦ *No dogs allowed* ♦ *Parking facilities : rue Clauzel and boulevard Rochechouart* ♦ *Transportation : Metro stations Saint-Georges or Pigalle - Buses 30, 54, 67 and 74.*

Now people begin to discover the 9th arrondissement. With its squares, private residences, theatres, and streets with buildings from the 1830s with white shutters, it is one of Paris most charming districts. The little rue Navarin is like this ; you can feel the countryside, thanks to the gardens which you'll discover by pushing the doors to the buildings. The same goes for the Hôtel de Navarin et d'Angleterre which hides behind its walls a garden with two huge locust trees, a big ivy and flower beds, where breakfast is served in the summer.

This hotel has just been renovated, and its small living room with good sofas and armchairs of Louis-Philippe style, freshened by light curtains showing soft blue prints is a success. A family dining room opens onto the garden. The rooms are very simple : wallpapers with tiny flowers and naïve wall lamps ; they are brightened up by silky red, blue or yellow curtains. Very clean bathrooms which take up some of the room's space as it used to be done in the past. Modest even in its prices, this hotel is meant for people who don't have delusions of grandeur.

Hôtel Excelsior ★★

16 rue Caroline - 75017 Paris
Tel. : (1) 45 22 50 95
Manager : Mr Le Ralle

♦ *22 sound-proofed rooms with shower or bath, TV, hair-drier, direct dial line* ♦ *Garden* ♦ *Prices : single with shower or bath : 350 F ; double with shower or bath : 450 F - Extra bed : 70 F* ♦ *Breakfast with orange juice : 27 F* ♦ *Off-season : weekends and December to February* ♦ *Credit cards : American Express and Visa* ♦ *Facilities : reservations, laundry, dry-cleaning* ♦ *Dogs allowed* ♦ *Transportation : Metro stations Rome or Place-Clichy - Buses 30, 53, 54, 66, 68, 74, 80, 81 and 95.*

It is always surprising to notice that in Paris a street or a boulevard are real frontiers between two totally different worlds. This is the case for the boulevard des Batignolles which closes the business area surrounding the Saint-Lazare train station. Further on begins a residential district with small squares and quiet streets.

The rue Caroline is one of them, and the Excelsior is a hotel that goes perfectly well with the district : welcoming, in all simplicity.

Soft lights, large sandstone tiles, Louis XIII furniture among which a Breton cupboard (a family keepsake) sits imposingly in the entrance. Comfortable rooms with fluffy blue, green or grey moquette where the rustic furniture is particularly pretty. Small, impeccable bathrooms.

The surprise comes from the garden on which give over half of the rooms, and a fig tree which you can see from the two ground floor rooms.

Because of this little garden, the smiles and the moderate rates, this is a very good address.

Ermitage Hôtel ★★

24 rue Lamarck - 75018 Paris
Tel. : (1) 42 64 79 22 - Fax : (1) 42 64 10 33
Managers : Mr and Mrs Canipel

*◆ 12 rooms with shower or bath, direct dial line ◆ Small garden ;
no lift or breakfast room ◆ Prices : single : 310 F ; double :
360 F ; triple : 450 F ◆ Breakfast included ◆ No off-season ◆ No
credit cards accepted ◆ Facilities : reservations ◆ Small dogs
allowed ◆ Parking facilities : 20 rue Lamarck ◆ Transportation :
Metro stations Lamarck-Caulaincourt or Château-Rouge - Buses
64, 80 or 85, Montmartre minibus and funicular of the Sacré-Cœur.*

This is a two-storey white house with tiny wrought iron balconies, it
is located 200 yards away from the Sacré-Cœur but is totally calm
in a district which still looks like a village and where people know
each other. When you are in the blue entrance hall, you can see
through the kitchen door an Alsacian ceramic stove. Further on, in
the lounge a Provençal kneading-trough and little fireplace giving
warmth and light in winter. This hotel can be summed up by saying
that it shows a taste for gay and pretty things. Ceramics, painted
mirrors and small Italian scenes decorate the landings. The rooms
are very much like those inhabited by our grandmothers, they are
full of souvenirs held by the printed fabrics showing flowers or
birds, the cosy beds and the period wardrobes, some marquetry or
walnut wood cane piece and always a little armchair and a good
desk. If you want to benefit from the trees, the terraces of the two
ground floor rooms and the "super panorama" wallpaper showing
views of Paris, you should stay in a room on the garden side.
However the front rooms are just as charming. This is an old-
fashioned hotel where happiness will cost you close to nothing.

Hôtel Prima-Lepic ★★

29 rue Lepic - 75018 Paris
Tel. : (1) 46 06 44 64 - Telex : 281 162 - Fax : (1) 46 06 66 11
Manager : Mrs Renouf

♦ *35 rooms and 3 suites, sound-proofed on the street side, with bath, direct dial line and TV* ♦ *Prices : single : 260 to 290 F ; double : 290 to 340 F ; triple : 380 to 500 F ; suite : 500 to 600 F* ♦ *Breakfast with orange juice, cheese and different sorts of Viennese pastries : 32 F* ♦ *Off-season : January and February (exclusive of professional shows)* ♦ *Credit card : Visa* ♦ *Facilities : reservations* ♦ *No dogs allowed* ♦ *Parking facilities : impasse Marie-Blanche* ♦ *Transportation : Metro stations Blanche or Abbesses - Buses 80 and Montmartre minibus.*

Near the Moulin de la Galette, this hotel starts with a large lobby followed by a sitting room decorated like a winter garden, it is overwhelmed by green plants, with over-elaborated furniture in white wrought iron. Steep and narrow stairs go up to the first floor and a large colour photo pinned on the wall completes this fresh and unpretentious decoration. In an adjoining sitting room, a curious but very original decoration is created by a beautiful fresco showing Montmartre as it used to be, a sofa Empire style, a writing desk and a funny little marble fireplace decorated with moon crescents, swords, salamandres and griffons. The rooms are a bit like the ground floor : impeccable flowered wallpaper with matching plain cotton curtains and bedspreads. They would seem ordinary but for an old bedside table or a straw-bottomed chair adding a little character. Notice room #55, furnished in art deco style and the larger front rooms, where a sitting room corner has often been arranged.

A cosy, well kept hotel which has a certain originality, and is located in one of Paris nicest districts.

Hôtel Regyn's Montmartre ★★

18 place des Abbesses - 75018 Paris
Tel. : (1) 42 54 45 21 - Telex : 650 269 - Fax : (1) 42 54 45 21
Manager : Mr Cadin

♦ *22 rooms, sound-proofed on the street side, with shower or bath, direct dial line, TV and hair-drier* ♦ *Prices : single : 325 to 345 F ; double : 380 to 400 F - Extra bed : 65 F* ♦ *Breakfast with cheese : 32 F* ♦ *Off-season : January, February and August* ♦ *Credit cards : Eurocard, MasterCard and Visa* ♦ *Facilities : reservations, laundry, dry-cleaning* ♦ *Dogs allowed* ♦ *Parking facilities : 3 rue des Abbesses and 5 rue Dancourt* ♦ *Transportation : Metro station Abbesses - Buses 30, 54, 67 and Montmartre minibus.*

A trompe-l'œil shows pink and blue clouds seen through fake windows, the furniture is white bistro style, this is the fresh decoration of this hotel's ground floor where a small entrance leads to a dining room-lounge.
Depending on the floor, the rooms are salmon pink, pale pink or beige. They are light and cosy with pretty cork panelled and white tiled bathrooms. If you want to benefit from the trees growing on the place des Abbesses, take a room whose number ends with 4, 6 or 8 ; the others give on the square.
A young staff, a warm welcome, this is a nice little hotel.

Terrass Hôtel ★★★★

12-14 rue Joseph-de-Maistre - 75018 Paris
Tel. : (1) 46 06 72 85 - Telex : 280 830 - Fax : (1) 42 52 29 11
Manager : Mr Binet

♦ *101 sound-proofed rooms and suites with bath, direct dial line, TV by satellite, hair-drier and minibar* ♦ *Terrace on the roof, bar, restaurants "Le Guerlande" and "L'Albatros", conference rooms* ♦ *Prices : single : 760 F ; double : 900 F ; air-conditioned suite : 1 250 F - Extra bed : 450 F* ♦ *Breakfast : 60 F* ♦ *Off-season : winter (exclusive of professional shows)* ♦ *Credit cards : Air+, American Express, Diners, En Route, JCB and Visa* ♦ *Facilities : all those of its category, snacks* ♦ *Dogs allowed* ♦ *Parking facilities : by carrier and impasse Marie-Blanche* ♦ *Transportation : Metro station Place-Clichy - Buses 54, 68, 74, 80, 81 and 95.*

Built at the bottom of the Butte Montmartre by the owner's great-grand-father, the building overhangs the trees of Montmartre cemetary and the rest of Paris. Its gorgeous green terrace makes you forget you are in an outlying part of Paris. Carefully kept up, it presents all the characteristics of French hotels. In the rooms, of a 1930s style, dressing tables and davenports are embeded in oak wainscotting. Ginger-coloured panelling, checkered moquette and plain 1950s curtains. Rustic furniture and flowered prints, or alcoves and furniture either Charles X or Louis-Philippe for the 1960-70s rooms. Light wood, sharp lines and soft prints for the rooms on the upper floors which have just been renovated. A lot of light, in particular on the street side (south) and most quiet on the other side. All the rooms are impeccable, so are the bathrooms. The lobby is disappointing but the bar is pretty with its large stone fireplace. The menus show the imagination of the chef, both at "Le Guerlande" and "L'Albatros" (quicker). And in the summer you can eat out on the terrace.

TimHôtel Montmartre ★★

11 rue Ravignan - 75018 Paris
Tel. : (1) 42 55 74 79 - Telex : 650 508 - Fax : (1) 42 55 71 01
Manager : Mr Paini

♦ *64 rooms with shower or bath, direct dial line, TV and video ;
baby-bottle-heater, cradle, iron and ironing board upon request*
♦ *Conference room* ♦ *Prices : single with shower : 290 F, with
bath : 375 F ; double with bath : 400 F - Extra bed : 100 F*
♦ *Breakfast with fruit and cheese : 32 F* ♦ *Off-season : winter
(exclusive of professional shows)* ♦ *Credit cards : American
Express, Diners and Visa* ♦ *Facilities : reservations* ♦ *Dogs
allowed* ♦ *Parking facilities : impasse Marie-Blanche and 3 rue
des Abbesses* ♦ *Transportation : Metro station Abbesses - Buses
30, 54, 67, 80 and Montmartre minibus.*

The hotel is wonderfully located on the heights of Montmartre on a
quiet, shaded square lost in the middle of public squares and
surrounded by steep flights of stairs tumbling down the hill...
This hotel which has Paris to its feet is by far the most agreeable of
the TimHôtel group. A warm welcome and a striking view. And,
since this year, blue or pink hangings cover the walls of all the
rooms and blue curtains brighten up a decoration which wasn't the
nicest part of this establishment.
Ask for a room overlooking the square, they all give on trees and on
the top floor they have a view on the roofs surrounding the Sacré-
Cœur. The fourth and fifth floor front rooms offer the most beautiful
view of Paris. For those who are not scared away by tarnished
colours and wall moquette, this comfortable hotel is charming.

146

Iris Hôtel ★★

80 rue de la Folie-Regnault - 75011 Paris
Tel. : (1) 43 57 73 30 - Telex : 211 094 - Fax : (1) 47 00 38 29
Managers : Messrs Laechler and Huynh

♦ *33 sound-proofed rooms with bath, direct dial line and TV*
♦ *Mini-patio* ♦ *Prices : single : 400 F ; double : 450 F - Extra bed : 120 F* ♦ *Breakfast with fruit juice and cheese : 30 F* ♦ *Off-season : January to March and August* ♦ *Credit cards : American Express, Diners and Visa* ♦ *Facilities : reservations, laundry, dry-cleaning, snacks* ♦ *Dogs allowed* ♦ *Parking facilities : Renault garage, rue du Chemin-Vert* ♦ *Transportation : Metro station Père-Lachaise, RER Nation - Buses 61 and 69.*

The hotel was renovated in the autumn of 1989, and it is a great surprise in this district where the streets bear rural names and where you can visit Paris most beautiful cemetary.

On the ground floor, the decoration shows in a very pleasant way the mixed origins of the hotel's owners : the Chinese refinement of Mr Huynh and the Swiss rigour of Mr Laechler. Big grey and white shining tiles, black leather sofas and large mirrors highlight a Pekinese panelling of painted irises, faience seats and a Buddha of white porcelain. In the back, around the living room corner, you'll find a beautifully flowered patio with just enough room to hold one table and one chair. The rooms are simple, grey or pink whether on the street side (larger) or overlooking the courtyard ; furniture of painted wood in matching tones, and always a place to write. The bathrooms are modern, tiled in white. An excellent little hotel fully deserving its 2 stars.

Nouvel-Hôtel ★★

24 avenue du Bel-Air - 75012 Paris
Tel. : (1) 43 43 01 81 - Telex : 240 139 - Fax : (1) 43 44 64 13
Managers : Mr and Mrs Marillier

♦ *28 sound-proofed rooms with washbasins, shower or bath, direct dial line and* TV ♦ *Patio and garden* ♦ *Prices : single or double with washbasins : 230 F, with shower : 330 F, with bath : 340 to 460 F ; triple : 480 F* ♦ *Breakfast with orange juice, fresh fruits and cheese : 37 F* ♦ *Off-season : July and August* ♦ *Credit cards : American Express, Diners and Visa* ♦ *Facilities : reservations, laundry, dry-cleaning* ♦ *Dogs allowed* ♦ *Parking facilities : 24 avenue de Saint-Mandé* ♦ *Transportation : Metro station and RER Nation - Buses 56, 62 and 86 ; 351 to Roissy Airport.*

Rue du Pensionnat, avenue du Bel-Air, rue Fabre-d'Eglantine, rue des Colonnes-du-Trône, these are reminiscences of a rural Paris (and of its history, from Louis XIV to the Revolution). Surrounded by trees, the Nouvel-Hôtel witnesses this rural past : three buildings surround a patio and a garden separated by sumptuous wistaria, lattice work, bamboo and flowers. On the party wall, imposing ivy forms a refuge for the birds of the district. Mr and Mrs Marillier managed to keep the atmosphere of this place. Renovated with care, the living-dining room still has a garland of fruits from the 1920s ; and the rooms have not lost their charm when bathrooms (small, but well equipped) were installed : rustic or exotic, all are agreeable. But remember room #127, blue, #129, opening onto the patio, and rooms bearing numbers in 1, 4, 6 or 8 which really take advantage of the garden... A family hotel where you are welcomed with care and offering satisfying breakfasts (a complete range of China teas and candy sugar). The bill is not excessive.

Because there are Sunday evenings when one would gladly breathe in country air before a candlelight dinner in front of a log-fire, we made room in *Paris - A Guide to Hotels of Charm* for pretty weekend outing places which we chose for their proximity ant their touristic interest : in the forests (Fontainebleau, Rambouillet, Chantilly and Compiègne), along rivers (Oise, Marne, Seine...), near golf courts (Le Tremblay-sur-Mauldre), or in State protected areas (regional park of the Vallée de Chevreuse, Moret-sur-Loing, Monfort-l'Amaury...).

This also shows in the classification we chose, it seems to us most suggestive. Inns, mills, castles, here are, within less than an hour from Paris, 23 addresses where to go when you feel romantic...

Hôtel Le Prieuré ★★★

Chevêt de l'Eglise
60440 Ermenonville (Oise)
Tel. : 44 54 00 44 - Telex : 145 110
Managers : Mr and Mrs Treillou

♦ *Closed in February* ♦ *10 rooms, sound-proofed on the street side, with shower or bath, direct dial line, TV and minibar* ♦ *Garden, paved courtyard, bar* ♦ *Prices : single or double with shower : 450 F, with bath : 500 F* ♦ *Breakfast : 40 F* ♦ *Credit card : Visa* ♦ *Small dogs allowed* ♦ *Transportation : 50 km northeast of Paris by A 1 exit Survilliers, then take D 922.*

Bowers, clematis, roses and hardy perennial, this English garden hides behind its walls the most beautiful hotel of the area : an old priory where the masters of the house allied their taste for beautiful objects to a sense of comfort.

On the ground floor, a serie of linked living rooms, each with a fireplace, a corner to read or write, large French windows opening onto the garden. In the rooms of tendre shades, we liked the soft quilted bedspreads with beautiful prints, the polished wood of the old wardrobes, and the beams in the attic rooms.

From top to bottom, this house pleases the eye : paintings, trinkets, sheened period pieces on polished floortiles and pretty rugs. It is simply charming.

No restaurant, but it doesn't matter, the countryside is gorgeous and you'll find nice places for dinner.

♦ *What to do : park and forest of Ermenonville with the Sand Sea ; abbey of Châalis, castle of Raray where Cocteau filmed "The Beauty and the Beast" (18-hole golf court), royal city of Senlis ; observation of stags in September, walks and riding in the forest.*

Auberge de Fontaine ★★

22 Grande Rue
Fontaine-Châalis - 60300 Senlis (Oise)
Tel. : 44 54 20 22
Managers : Mr and Mrs Campion

♦ *Closed in February, on Tuesdays and Wednesdays (except in September, October and November)* ♦ *9 rooms with washbasins, shower or bath, direct dial line* ♦ *Shaded terrace, little garden, bar, restaurant* ♦ *Prices : single or double with washbasins : 180 F, with shower : 230 F, with bath : 260 F* ♦ *Breakfast with orange juice : 26 F* ♦ *Credit card : Visa* ♦ *No dogs allowed* ♦ *Transportation : 50 km northeast of Paris by A 1 exit Saint-Witz, then take D 126, D 922 via Mortefontaine and D 126 through the forest of Ermenonville.*

Near the forest, the little hotel de Fontaine is a quite pleasant place.
A terrace and a tiny garden, two large fireplaces and flowered curtains give atmosphere to this inn managed with an obvious pleasure.
Mr Campion is in the kitchen and Mrs Campion takes care of the hotel. For the rooms she chose flowered wallpapers of pink or blue shades which stand out well on the exposed beams, lace for the windows and brown wood furniture with round flapped tables. Very clean and bright, these are true countryside bedrooms.
A good smell of hot pie fills the ground floor and is a good sign for the coming meal. A very simple place, with much quality.

♦ *What to do : park and forest of Ermenonville with the Sand Sea ; abbey of Châalis, castle of Raray where Cocteau filmed "The Beauty and the Beast" (18-hole golf court), royal city of Senlis ; observation of stags in September, walks and riding in the forest.*

Hostellerie du Pavillon Saint-Hubert ★★

Toutevoie - 60270 Gouvieux (Oise)
Tel. : 44 57 07 04 - Fax : (1) 44 57 75 42
Manager : Mr Luck

♦ *Closed from 15 January to 15 February* ♦ *22 rooms with shower or bath, direct dial line, (12 with TV and minibar)* ♦ *Garden, shaded terrace on the Oise river, bar, restaurant* ♦ *Prices : single or double with shower (no WC) : 150 F, with shower: 220 F, with bath : 240 F* ♦ *Breakfast : 30 F* ♦ *Credit cards : American Express and Visa* ♦ *Dogs allowed* ♦ *Transportation : 55 km northeast of Paris by A 1 exit Saint-Witz, then take N 17 and D 924a to Chantilly, then D 909 to Gouvieux ; 4 km from Gouvieux.*

A few kilometers away from the riding paths disappearing into the forest, the Pavillon Saint-Hubert is a very attractive alternative to the so civilized cottages and lawns of Chantilly.

Closed to be renovated after a change of managers, this completely white house has just reopened... and gives the delicious impression of an old time inn where nothing has changed.

Country-like, out of the way, but overlooking the river, the hotel is warmed up by beams, wainscot, and brick fireplaces. The copperware sparkles, the pink tablecloth invite you to taste the chef's cooking. All the rooms are on the first floor, wallpaper with small flowers, light-coloured bedspreads, comfortable and pretty furniture. Through the flounced net curtains you can see the barges gliding closeby. In the summer, tables are set on the grass to benefit from the quiet, the river and the sunshine. The managers, who are no new-comers in the business, created here a hotel with atmosphere where the welcome is full of smiles.

♦ *What to do : forest and castle of Chantilly, races, abbey of Royaumont, royal city of Senlis, auction sales in Senlis and Compiègne ; walks, riding, golf.*

A la Bonne Idée ★★★

60350 Saint-Jean-aux-Bois (Oise)
Tel. : 44 42 84 09 / 44 42 82 64 - Telex : 155 026
Manager : Mr Royer

♦ *Closed from 15 January to 15 February and the last week of August* ♦ *24 rooms with bath, direct dial line and TV* ♦ *Restaurant* ♦ *Prices : double : 390 F* ♦ *Breakfast : 47 F* ♦ *Credit cards : American Express, Eurocard, MasterCard and Visa* ♦ *Dogs allowed* ♦ *Transportation : 75 km northeast of Paris by A 1 exit Verberie, then take D 932a via Lacroix-Saint-Ouen and D 85 through the forest of Compiègne .*

An old 17th century harbour master's office, this inn is located in a cute little village, at the heart of the forest of Compiègne. In the first living room and the bar, modern and period pieces are matched. The beautiful dining room is a perfect setting for the excellent cooking prepared by the chef and owner.

As for the rooms, you can choose between those in the main building, old and full of charm, or those in the small annexe opening onto the flowered garden and the shaded terrace. In both cases, they are perfectly arranged. The very amiable welcome and the quietness thanks to its location in a dead-end street are just as many other reasons to like this address, one hour away from Paris.

♦ *What to do : castle of Pierrefonds, auction sales in Compiègne ; swimming pool, tennis, fishing, walks.*

Hostellerie Le Gonfalon ★★★

2 rue de l'Eglise
77910 Germigny-l'Evêque (Seine-et-Marne)
Tel. : (1) 64 33 16 05
Manager : Mrs Colubi

♦ *Closed in January, on Sunday evenings and Mondays* ♦ *10 rooms with shower or bath, direct dial line and TV* ♦ *Garden, terrace, landing stage on the Marne river, private terraces or winter gardens, bar, restaurant* ♦ *Prices : single or double : 300 to 340 F* ♦ *Breakfast with homemade buns and fruit juices : 40 F* ♦ *Credit cards : American Express, Diners and Visa* ♦ *Dogs allowed* ♦ *Transportation : 60 km east of Paris by A 4 until Meaux, then take N 3 to Trilport and D 97.*

A few kilometers away from Meaux, Mrs Colubi skillfully manages a pretty hotel ; a family mansion standing in the shade, in a loop of the Marne river.

An imposing stone fireplace divides the space of the ground floor, the biggest side was alloted to the restaurant, entirely blue, even the candles in the silver candelabras.

A lot of people come here for the food, which made the renown of the hostess. But it also is a pleasure to live in this hotel where everything was carefully thought out to provide with an extremely comfortable and peaceful stay. The best rooms are those with private winter gardens overlooking the trees along the Marne river. And when the sun shines on the river, you won't resist to the pleasure of a drink or to taste the homemade buns sitting at a table by the river.

♦ *What to do : walks and cycling in the forest of Montceaux, golf, sightseeing on the Marne river.*

Auberge du Moulin de Jarcy ★★

**50 rue Boieldieu
91480 Varennes-Jarcy (Essonne)
Tel. : (1) 69 00 89 20
Manager : Mr Le Moign**

♦ *Closed from 1 to 22 August and from 22 December to 15 January (rooms available only on weekends)* ♦ *5 rooms with washbasins* ♦ *Restaurant (closed on Wednesdays and Thursdays)* ♦ *Prices : single or double : 150 to 200 F* ♦ *Breakfast : 30 F* ♦ *Credit cards : Eurocard, MasterCard and Visa* ♦ *No dogs allowed* ♦ *Transportation : 28 km southeast of Paris by N 19 (Pont-de-Charenton) until Villecresne, then take D 33e to Mandres-les-Roses and D 53 via Périgny.*

At less than 30 kilometers from Paris, along the Yerres river, the Moulin de Jarcy is a 12th century old windmill with its paddle wheels and machinery. Well restored, the five attic rooms were arranged in a rustic style. The winter dining room, wherefrom you'll catch a glimpse of the mill's wheel, still working, is a nice setting to taste good cuisine, changing according to the seasons. Like for all hotel-restaurants near Paris, take care to book if you want to stay a weekend or lunch on a Sunday.

The rooms are available only on weekends.

♦ *What to do : castle of Vaux-le-Vicomte ; walks in the forest of Sénart ; riding, tennis, golf, fishing with a licence.*

Hôtel Legris et Parc ★★★

36 rue du Parc
77300 Fontainebleau (Seine-et-Marne)
Tel. : (1) 64 22 24 24 - Telex : 692 131 - Fax : (1) 64 22 22 05
Manager : Mr Mary

♦ *Closed in January* ♦ *24 rooms and 6 suites, sound-proofed on the street side, with shower or bath, direct dial line and TV* ♦ *Large garden, private terraces, conference rooms, bar, restaurant (closed on Sunday evenings from October to March)* ♦ *Prices : single or double with shower : 250 F, with bath : 340 to 400 F ; suite : 350 to 500 F* ♦ *Breakfast : 35 F* ♦ *Credit cards : Diners and Visa* ♦ *Dogs allowed* ♦ *Transportation : 65 km southeast of Paris by A 6.*

Fontainebleau shelters many hotels. The Legris et Parc has the qualities of a traditional hotel : an ideal location (it stands against the castle and at the entrance of the park), perfect quiet (the hotel is mostly turned towards the big garden), faultless comfort (rooms are spacious, well furnished and very light on the garden side), last but not least a skilled staff.

This 17th century old town house also has style. In the restaurant, the silverware and the round lamps look very pretty on the white tablecloth. In the rooms, mirrors, canopies, 17th century chests of drawers are in perfect harmony with the blue, yellow or light-brown decoration.

But the marvellous part is the garden with a big chalet built at the beginning of the century which can be booked for receptions, and the chestnut trees casting their shade on the lawns.

♦ *What to do : castles of Fontainebleau and Vaux-le-Vicomte ; cycling and walks in the forest of Fontainebleau, swimming pool, riding, golf.*

Hostellerie du Country-Club ★★★

**11 quai Franklin-Roosevelt
77920 Samois-sur-Seine (Seine-et-Marne)
Tel. : (1) 64 24 60 34 - Telex : 690 247
Manager : Mr Plançon**

♦ *Closed for Christmas, on Sunday evenings and Mondays*
♦ *15 rooms with shower or bath, direct dial line and* TV ♦ *Garden,*
terrace, private terraces, tennis ♦ *Prices : single or double : 300*
to 360 F ♦ *Breakfast : 35 F* ♦ *Credit card : Visa* ♦ *No dogs*
allowed ♦ *Transportation : 75 km southeast of Paris by A 6 to*
Fontainebleau, then take D 210 and D 137 along the left bank of
the Seine.

Houses and chalets from the beginning of the century, fishermen,
landing stages, tiny islands and restaurants : the banks of the Seine
in Samois still have charm, and it is great to find a hotel where to
live a few days to the rythm of time past.
Round picture windows, private terraces, a restaurant overlooking
the garden : the hotel gives on the river which slowly flows by, on
the other side of a small road down below. Mr Plançon was as
careful with the restaurant than with the hotel, where the luminous
rooms, and comfortable bathrooms, are very nice.
Tennis and cycling for inveterate sportsmen, the forest paths for
walkers. A wonderful location, a very good hotel.

♦ *What to do : castles of Fontainebleau and Vaux-le-Vicomte,*
auction sales in Melun ; cycling and walks along the Seine and in
the forest of Fontainebleau ; riding, swimming pool, golf,
sightseeing on the river.

Auberge de la Terrasse ★★

40 rue de la Pêcherie
77250 Moret-sur-Loing (Seine-et-Marne)
Tel. : (1) 60 70 51 03
Managers : Mr and Mrs Mignon

♦ *20 rooms with shower or bath, direct dial line, (14 with TV)*
♦ *Terrace, bar, restaurant (closed on Sunday evenings and Mondays)* ♦ *Prices : single with shower : 185 and 225 F, with bath : 310 F ; double with shower : 250 and 295 F, with bath : 340 F* ♦ *Breakfast : 31 F* ♦ *Credit card : Visa* ♦ *Dogs allowed* ♦ *Transportation : 70 km southeast of Paris by A 6 to Fontainebleau, then take N 6.*

Moret-sur-Loing is a medieval town which has kept inside its walls the character of bygone days. Sisley and Clémenceau did not miss it, they lived here ; neither did Mr and Mrs Mignon : they took over the hotel two years ago and transformed it into an excellent place where to stop.
The wooden bar is splendid, beams and a fireplace where a fire crackles in the winter. You will pass the time there before having dinner (promising) in the restaurant overlooking the river : tables set in blue and imposing stone fireplace. When they are renovated (the majority) the rooms also are blue, country-like and clean as a new pin, not big but comfortable. Impeccable tiled bathrooms.
To people who would be scared away by the Moret festival (the hotel sees it all), we advise to go spend the evening nearby : at midnight, silence overwhelms the town again.

♦ *What to do : castle of Fontainebleau ; walks, riding, sightseeing on the river.*

Hôtel de la Vanne Rouge ★★

77690 Montigny-sur-Loing (Seine-et-Marne)
Tel. : (1) 64 45 82 10
Managers : Mr and Mrs Porta

♦ *Closed from 10 January to March, from Sunday evening to Tuesday morning from October to April, on Mondays from May to October* ♦ *11 rooms with shower or bath* ♦ *Large terrace overlooking the Loing river, bar, restaurant* ♦ *Prices : single or double : 180 to 250 F - Extra bed : 30 F* ♦ *Breakfast : 28 F* ♦ *Credit card : Visa* ♦ *Dogs allowed* ♦ *Transportation : 70 km southeast of Paris by A 6 to Fontainebleau, then take N 7 and D 58.*

This big chalet with a tower and half-timbering almost touches the water. Mr and Mrs Porta created a wonderful shaded terrace where only the water murmur and the birds singing can be heard. In the summer good cooking is served there ; and in the winter you can take advantage of it from the dining room, intimate with its fire, and where most of the windows give on the river.
Blue, pink, flowers, painted wood or brass furniture, cotton or lace bedspreads, the rooms are "just like at home", and delicious.
A kind welcome, even Roméo the grey parrot posted at the entrance says "Au revoir et merci!".

♦ *What to do : castles of Montigny and Fontainebleau ; cycling and walks in the forest of Fontainebleau, riding, sightseeing on the river.*

Auberge "Le Pied Jaloux"

1 rue Pasteur
77116 Recloses (Seine-et-Marne)
Tel. : (1) 64 24 20 04
Managers : Mr and Mrs Gilbert-Collet

♦ *Closed from mid-December to mid-March, on Wednesdays and Thursdays (except on public holidays)* ♦ *4 rooms with shower or bath* ♦ *Large terrace with swimming pool, shaded courtyard, restaurant* ♦ *Prices : single or double : 250 F - Extra bed : 30 F* ♦ *Breakfast : 30 F* ♦ *Credit card : Visa* ♦ *Dogs allowed* ♦ *Transportation : 75 km southeast of Paris by A 6 exit Ury, then take D 63e.*

Recloses with its sturdy little church, the elm trees on the square, its quiet alleys, is a beautiful village and a pretty place where to break your journey if you want to benefit from the forest of Fontainebleau. At " Le Pied Jaloux", a large willow tree stands erect in the paved courtyard and invites you to climb the steps leading to the main building. Then you discover an immense terrace where tables are set during the summer and... a swimming pool refreshing after a day spent in the forest.

Four rooms (not one more, what a dream!) to sleep in peace, impeccable white bathrooms, a dining room with a brick fireplace : a charming hotel, youthful and gay.

♦ *What to do : castles of Bourron-Marlotte and Fontainebleau, rocks of Recloses, sand-quarry in Bourron ; cycling and walks in the forest of Fontainebleau, riding, golf, sightseeing on the river.*

Auberge Casa del Sol ★★

**63 rue des Canches
77116 Recloses (Seine-et-Marne)
Tel. : (1) 64 24 20 35 - Telex : 692 131
Manager : Mrs Hude-Courcoul**

♦ *Closed from 20 December to 1 February, and on Tuesday evenings off-season* ♦ *10 rooms with washbasins, shower or bath, direct dial line and TV* ♦ *Restaurant* ♦ *Prices : single : 230 F ; double : 310 to 350 F ; suite : 550 F* ♦ *Breakfast : 35 F* ♦ *Credit cards : American Express, Diners and Visa* ♦ *Dogs allowed* ♦ *Transportation : 75 km southeast of Paris by A 6 exit Ury, then take D 63e.*

Forty minutes away from Paris, and 10 minutes from Fontainebleau, a pretty flowered old house, with modest proportions, and well restored.

The rooms are smart and comfortable, the style rustic ; some are slightly isolated, in the attic ; all are very quiet.

Recent transformations changed the dining room and the living room for the better. In the summer, the meals are served on the terrace. The cuisine is both traditional and modern, using fresh products of the area. Colette Courcoul, the owner, very attentionate and dynamic, creates a gay and friendly atmosphere in her inn.

♦ *What to do : castles of Bourron-Marlotte and Fontainebleau, rocks of Recloses, sand-quarry in Bourron ; cycling and walks in the forest of Fontainebleau, riding, golf, sightseeing on the river.*

Hôtel Les Alouettes ★★

4 rue Antoine-Barye
77630 Barbizon (Seine-et-Marne)
Tel. : (1) 60 66 41 98 - Telex : 693 580 - Fax : (1) 60 66 20 69
Managers : Mr and Mrs Cresson

♦ *20 rooms and 2 suites with shower or bath, direct dial line*
♦ *Large garden, terrace, tennis, bar, restaurant (closed on Sunday evenings)* ♦ *Prices : single or double : 220 to 330 F ; suite : 350 to 390 F* ♦ *Breakfast : 30 F* ♦ *Credit cards : American Express, Diners and Visa* ♦ *Dogs allowed* ♦ *Transportation : 45 km southeast of Paris by A 6 exit towards Fontainebleau, then take N 37.*

Barbizon became well knowed thanks to painters who moved there to work, it now looks like a village you'd see in a light opera, invaded by tourists during the summer. With the forest nearby, of a modest size and still pretty, this village has a lot of charm if you can avoid the weekends or if you take the precautions to stay in a more isolated place ; at the Alouettes for example, a house built by the brothers Seailles in the middle of the last century to welcome their friends and painters. This friendly resort atmosphere is still there and gives all its quality to this hotel where every rememberance of the past was maintained with love : large library in a sunlit living room, delicat still lifes painted directly on the doors, paintings and period pieces in the corridors, country-like and comfortable rooms giving on the garden.

A gourmet cooking, a kind welcome : it is understandable that the hotel should often be full.

♦ *What to do : castles of Fontainebleau and Courances, Milly-la-Forêt ; walks in the forest of Fontainebleau, riding, swimming pool, golf.*

Le Moulin de Flagy ★★★

2 rue du Moulin
77940 Flagy (Seine-et-Marne)
Tel. : (1) 60 96 67 89
Managers : Mr and Mrs Scheidecker

♦ *Closed on the last week of September, from 20 December to 22 January, on Sunday evenings and Mondays* ♦ *10 rooms with bath, direct dial line, (3 with TV)* ♦ *Restaurant (closed for Easter, Pentecost and 11 November)* ♦ *Prices : single : 180 to 200 F ; double : 235 to 390 F* ♦ *Breakfast : 35 F* ♦ *Credit cards : American Express, Diners, Eurocard, MasterCard and Visa* ♦ *Dogs allowed* ♦ *Transportation : 80 km southeast of Paris by A 6 to Fontainebleau, then take N 6 until Moret-sur-Loing, D 218 to Villecerf and D 22.*

This old 12th century mill was well restored. Under the roughcast, the machinery is still in very good shape, so were the original half-timbering, the tiles covered with cob, the exposed stones of the ground floor and the gable with its pretty vault. It now has a new vocation, with ten rooms of character and very comfortable, a dining room giving on the river, a terrace and a garden. Candlelight dinner is offered in the evening with, in winter, a hearty fire.
One hour from Paris you'll find here comfort and a quiet countryside.

♦ *What to do : golf of the Forteresse 3 km away, swimming pool, tennis, fishing.*

Hostellerie de Villemartin ★★★

4 allée des Marronniers
Villemartin - 91150 Morigny (Essonne)
Tel. : (1) 64 94 63 54
Manager : Mr Savignet

♦ *Closed in August, Sunday evenings and Mondays (excluding public holydays)* ♦ *14 rooms with washbasins, shower or bath, direct dial line and* TV ♦ *Restaurant, tennis* ♦ *Prices : single : 260 to 350 F ; double : 300 to 390 F* ♦ *Breakfast : 41 F* ♦ *Credit cards : American Express, Diners and Visa* ♦ *Dogs allowed* ♦ *Transportation : 45 km south of Paris by N 20 to Etréchy, then take D 17 towards Morigny ; locality of Villemartin.*

Side by side with a 16th century fortified farm, this charming manor house stands erect in the middle of a 17 hectares wooded park along the Juine river. Inside, the very classic decoration has less charm. Some of the large rooms, nicely renovated in a rustic style, open onto an Italian terrace where you can admire the park, splendid. The bathrooms are spacious and refined.
The cooking is of excellent quality and, at a candlelight dinner, you shall be able to savour the quietness of the place.
The welcome is very warm. An agreeable place to stop.

♦ *What to do : walks along the Juine river, Etampes ; riding, flying club, golf 4 km away.*

Auberge du Gros Marronnier ★★

**3 place de l'Eglise
78720 Senlisse (Yvelines)
Tel. : (1) 30 52 51 69 - Telex : 689 473
Manager : Mrs Trochon**

♦ *14 rooms with shower or bath, direct dial line* ♦ *Prices : double : 295 to 315 F* ♦ *Breakfast : 35 F* ♦ *Credit cards : American Express, Diners and Visa* ♦ *Dogs allowed* ♦ *Transportation : 53 km southwest of Paris by A 13 and A 12 to Versailles, then take N 10 to Maurepas et D 58 to Dampierre and Senlisse.*

In the regional park of the Vallée de Chevreuse, in one of the streets of Senlisse, stands this inn, as charming and simple as its name.

Once you are under the porch at the other end of the courtyard, you will see a splendid parish garden surrounded with walls, there you'll find fruit trees, a well, little benches and you'll have a view on the nearby church. A reassuring feelling of peaceful countryside, which you'll still find inside the house.

The rooms are tastefully decorated, all are different, in sizes, and details. The food, even if it is not the gastronomy of the Auberge du Pont Hardi, has the same qualities in flavour and its preparation. As soon as spring comes, you can benefit from the garden and listen to the chimes sitting at a table outside, in this heavenly corner.

♦ *What to do : abbey of Port-Royal, castles, Vallée de Chevreuse (regional parc), botanical garden, forest of Rambouillet ; riding, tennis.*

Auberge du Pont Hardi ★★★

1 rue du Couvent
78720 Senlisse (Yvelines)
Tel. : (1) 30 52 50 78 - Telex : 689 473
Manager : Mrs Trochon

♦ *Closed on Sunday evenings and Mondays* ♦ *6 rooms with shower or bath, direct dial line* ♦ *Restaurant* ♦ *Prices : single : 320 F ; double : 380 F* ♦ *Breakfast : 35 F* ♦ *Credit cards : American Express, Diners and Visa* ♦ *Dogs allowed* ♦ *Transportation : 53 km southwest of Paris by A 13 and A 12 to Versailles, then take N 10 to Maurepas and D 58 to Dampierre and Senlisse.*

Located in an alley of Senlisse, this ravishing old house has at its back vast and beautiful grounds, which you can appreciate all year round. As soon as the weather is nice, tables are set on a shaded terrace, but the large picture windows in the dining room (conventional Louis XIII decoration) allow you to see at all season the park's foliage.

The Auberge du Pont Hardi is, first of all, good cuisine. Eric Trochon was schooled by some of the best chefs and he prepares many traditional dishes, among which a delicious calf sweetbread with morels.

The few rooms are very comfortable, the careful decoration creates a soft atmosphere.

A nice address when you are looking for a relaxing and gastronomic weekend.

♦ *What to do : abbey of Port-Royal, castles, Vallée de Chevreuse (regional parc), botanical garden, forest of Rambouillet ; riding, tennis.*

Abbaye des Vaux de Cernay ★★★★

Cernay-la-Ville - 78720 Dampierre (Yvelines)
Tel. : (1) 34 85 23 00 - Telex : 689 596 - Fax : (1) 34 85 11 60
Manager : Mr Savry

♦ *60 rooms and 3 suites with bath, direct dial line and* TV
♦ *Wooded park of 65 hectares, pond, swimming pool, tennis,
reception rooms, bar, restaurant ; fishing, flights in hot air balloon,
private shoot, musical evenings* ♦ *Prices : single : 580 F ;
double : 790 to 990 F ; suite : 1 200 to 2 800 F* ♦ *Breakfast with
fruit juice and fresh fruit : 70 F* ♦ *Credit cards : American
Express, Diners and Visa* ♦ *Facilities : those of its category,
snacks* ♦ *Dogs allowed* ♦ *Transportation : 50 km southwest of
Paris by A 13 and A 12 to Versailles, then take N 10 to Maurepas
and D 58 towards Chevreuse.*

Right in the Vallée de Chevreuse, the estate of the abbey of Vaux de
Cernay is a world apart which shows up as if by magic in the thick
of the forest.
In the middle of the immense prairie cut into the woods, the abbey
spreads out its long convents enclosed on one side by the ruins of
the abbey-church. The hotel turned on the cloister's side shows an
incredible serie of lounges leading to the vaulted chapter house with
intersection of ribs. A gorgeous wistaria softens the austere lines of
the garden where you can sit in the shade of large white parasols.
The rooms ? They are just divine, and charm works even more in
the bathrooms enhanced by mosaics or sepia frescoes.
Out of this world, a splendid success.

♦ *What to do : castle and auction sales in Versailles, Vallée de
Chevreuse (regional park) ; riding, golf 9 km away.*

166

Château-hôtel du Tremblay-sur-Mauldre ★★★

78490 Montfort-l'Amaury (Yvelines)
Tel. : (1) 34 87 92 92 - Telex : 689 535 - Fax : (1) 34 87 88 23
Manager : Société hôtelière du Château du Tremblay

♦ *Closed from 24 to 30 December* ♦ *28 rooms with shower or bath, direct dial line, TV, minibar and fireplaces* ♦ *Park of 40 hectares, golf training (tutorials, training courses), 9-hole golf course and practice, terrace, bar, restaurant* ♦ *Prices : single or double : 450 to 1 100 F* ♦ *Breakfast with fruit juices : 45 F* ♦ *Credit cards : American Express, Diners and Visa* ♦ *Facilities : reservation, laundry, dry-cleaning* ♦ *Transportation : 40 km west of Paris by A 13 and A 12 to Versailles, then take N 12 et N 191.*

The forest of Rambouillet, the towns of Montfort-l'Amaury and Versailles : an exceptional location for this Louis XIII castle, just as exceptional as its immense park cut by valleys.
This country castle was restored two years ago with such dexterity that immediately charms the visitor.
Nothing flashy but always the right thing to tame the large proportions of the ground floor and the rooms. A very welcoming dark-blue living room corner around the fireplace, and a splendid marble console, a few paintings, the reflection of mirror doors dress the dining room, but most of all in front of the open windows with view on the park, long curtains of Indian silk with sumptuous colours. Same refined privacy in the sunlit rooms where in winter a fire is always kept burning when the night comes. A good address for golf lovers and an ideal stopping place for all the others.

♦ *What to do : castle and auction sales in Versailles, Thoiry nature reserve ; swimming pool, tennis, riding, walks in the forest of Rambouillet.*

Le Moulin d'Orgeval ★★★★

**Rue de l'Abbaye
78630 Orgeval (Yvelines)
Tel. : (1) 39 75 85 74 - Telex : 689 036 - Fax : (1) 39 75 48 52
Managers : Mr and Mrs Douvier**

♦ *14 rooms with shower or bath, direct dial line and TV* ♦ *Heated swimming pool, sauna, solarium, restaurant* ♦ *Prices : single : 480 F ; double : 650 F* ♦ *Breakfast : 50 F* ♦ *Credit cards : American Express, Diners, Eurocard, MasterCard and Visa* ♦ *Dogs allowed* ♦ *Transportation : 22 km west of Paris by A 13 exit Poissy-Villennes ; 2 km from Orgeval.*

The Moulin d'Orgeval is located along the river, at the heart of a 5 hectares flowered park. One of the islands in the middle of the park, is reserved to the birds.

This says how much this place can be pleasing, with its vegetation and quiet, only half an hour away from Paris (the bad side of this marvellous location : the hotel is very valued for receptions).

Here the 14 very comfortable rooms all overlook the park. In the rustic dining room, enlivened with a firewood grill, you'll be offered, depending on the season, all kinds of classic dishes.

♦ *What to do : Versailles, Saint-Germain-en-Laye (museum of national antiquities) ; tennis, riding, golf.*

Château de Brécourt ★★★★

27120 Douains (Eure)
Tel. : 32 52 40 50 - Telex : 172 250 - Fax : 32 52 69 65
Managers : Messrs Charpentier and Savry

♦ *25 rooms with bath, direct dial line* ♦ *Covered and heated swimming pool, jacuzzi, tennis, restaurant* ♦ *Prices : single : 600 F ; double : 850 F ; suite : 1 100 F* ♦ *Breakfast : 55 F* ♦ *Credit cards : American Express, Diners, Eurocard, MasterCard and Visa* ♦ *Dogs allowed* ♦ *Transportation : 75 km west of Paris by A 13 exit Vernon, then take D 75 towards Douains ; locality of Brécourt.*

At the doors of Normandy, the castle of Brécourt built at the time of Louis XIII is the ideal place for a weekend.

This beautiful 17th century castle, surrounded by moats, offers to its clients superb grounds of 22 hectares where it is good to walk at all season. Sports lovers will take advantage of the tennis courts and the swimming pool. To gourmets, two restaurant will serve Norman dishes, and offer a beautiful view on the woods and the countryside. The decoration is like the rest of the house : refined and very comfortable.

♦ *What to do : "route of castles and abbeys", Monet's house in Giverny.*

Hostellerie La Chaîne d'Or ★★

27 rue Grande
27700 Les Andelys (Eure)
Tel. : 32 54 00 31
Managers : Mr and Mrs Foucault

♦ *Closed in January, on Sunday evenings and Mondays from October to April* ♦ *12 rooms and suites with shower or bath, direct dial line* ♦ *Large shaded courtyard, terrace on the Seine river, bar, restaurant (open from April to October)* ♦ *Prices : single or double : 360 to 410 F ; suite : 770 F - Extra bed : 90 F* ♦ *Breakfast with orange juice : 45 F* ♦ *Credit card : Visa* ♦ *Small dogs allowed* ♦ *Transportation : 95 km west of Paris by A 13 exit Les Andelys, then take D 316 et D 313 ; locality of Petit-Andely.*

Les Andelys, it is already Normandy with the reminiscence of the Hundred-Year War and Château Gaillard stands erect on the top of the chalky cliff surmounting the Seine. The Chaîne d'Or is also part of this history, at the time when the city toll was paid in front of a chain… which was worth a lot of gold.

With a large flowered courtyard and overlooking the Seine, the hotel has kept the transformations that took place as time passed : annexes, terrace by the river, a glass gallery overwhelmed with flowers and trinkets. And the successful renovation lent some glamour to the very comfortable rooms, decorated in greyish blue or pink (we like particularly the older rooms, with their well polished wardrobes and long curtains of faded colours).

People come from far away to taste the cooking. This address is worth keeping in mind.

♦ *What to do : Château Gaillard, auction sales in Les Andelys, Monet's house in Giverny ; walks along the Seine river and in the forest, sightseeing on the river, swimming pool, tennis, riding, golf.*

Hôtel de Normandie ★

1 rue Grande
27700 Les Andelys (Eure)
Tel. : 32 54 10 52
Managers : Mr and Mrs Bourguignon

◆ *Closed in December, on Wednesday evenings and Thursdays*
◆ *11 rooms with washbasins, shower or bath, direct dial line,*
(6 with TV) ◆ *Garden on the Seine river, bar, restaurant* ◆ *Prices :*
single or double with washbasins : 130 F, with shower or bath :
250 F ◆ *Breakfast with fruit juice : 30 F* ◆ *Credit card : Visa*
◆ *Dogs allowed* ◆ *Transportation : 95 km northwest of Paris by*
A 13 exit Les Andelys, then take D 316 et D 313 ; locality of Petit-
Andely.

A one-floor corner house, the Hôtel de Normandie hides a beautiful
garden with pots of flowers and bowers covered with roses, and
giving on the Seine river.
A rustic decoration for the ground floor with small-paned doors,
corridors with green and white stripes where posters and little
paintings hang, very simple rooms where the bathrooms are
included in the space, here is an unpretentious hotel but very nice in
the summer.
For its odorous garden by the river and its unexpensive rates, this
place is well worth a stop.

◆ *What to do : Château Gaillard, auction sales in Les Andelys,*
Monet's house in Giverny ; walks along the Seine river and in the
forest, sightseeing on the river, swimming pool, tennis, riding, golf.

Index by *arrondissements*

8th arrondissement

9th arrondissement

11th arrondissement

12th arrondissement

13th arrondissement

14th arrondissement

15th arrondissement

16th arrondissement

17th arrondissement

18th arrondissement

Index by *départements*

Hotels in Paris
Alphabetical index

Hotels in outlying districts
Alphabetical index

Hotels in Paris
Price index

(First price for a double room - with shower or bath
❀ indicates hotels with a garden or a patio)

up to 300 F

Hôtel de Navarin et d'Angleterre ★★ (9th) ❀ : 280 F 140
Hôtel Esmeralda ★★ (5th) : 280 F 4
Hôtel des Grandes Ecoles ★★ (5th) ❀ : 280 F 15
Grand Hôtel des Balcons ★★ (6th) : 280 F 45
Hôtel Prima-Lepic ★★ (18th) : 290 F 143

from 300 to 400 F

Grand Hôtel Jeanne d'Arc ★★ (4th) : 300 F 129
Hôtel du Parc Montsouris ★★ (14th) : 300 F 23
Hôtel Plaisant ★★ (5th) : 320 F 14
Hôtel Brighton ★★★ (1st) : 330 F 117
Nouvel-Hôtel ★★ (12th) ❀ : 330 F 148
Hôtel de Nevers ★★ (7th) : 345 F 67
Résidence Les Gobelins ★★ (13th) ❀ : 350 F 22
Hôtel La Louisiane ★★ (6th) : 350 F 52
Hôtel Agora ★★ (1st) : 350 F 123
Hôtel du 7e Art ★★ (4th) : 360 F 127
Hôtel des Trois Collèges ★★ (5th) : 360 F 18
Hôtel du Jardin des Plantes ★★ (5th) : 360 F 20
Ermitage Hôtel ★★ (18th) ❀ : 360 F 142
Hôtel Sèvres-Azur ★★ (6th) : 370 F 36
Hôtel de la Tamise ★★★ (1st) : 370 F 116
Hôtel Beauvoir ★★ (5th) : 380 F 38
Hôtel Regyn's Montmartre ★★ (18th) : 380 F 144
Hôtel Ferrandi ★★★ (6th) : 385 F 34
Résidence du Pré ★★ (9th) : 395 F 136

from 400 to 500 F

Hôtel Saint-Merry ★★★ (4th) : 400 F 124
Hôtel des Célestins ★★ (4th) : 400 F 128
Hôtel des Saints-Pères ★★★ (6th) ❀ : 400 F 58
Hôtel Lecourbe ★★ (15th) ❀ : 400 F 75
Hôtel des Champs-Elysées ★★ (8th) : 400 F 102
TimHôtel Montmartre ★★ (18th) : 400 F 146
Hôtel Perreyve ★★ (6th) : 406 F 41
Hôtel de la Tulipe ★★ (7th) ❀ : 408 F 73
Hôtel Récamier ★★ (6th) : 410 F 41
Hôtel Louvre - Forum ★★★ (1st) : 410 F 122
Hôtel Beaubourg ★★★ (4th) : 430 F 125
Hôtel de Varenne ★★★ (7th) ❀ : 430 F 70
Hôtel Istria ★★ (14th) : 450 F 25
Hôtel des Deux Continents ★★ (6th) : 450 F 54
Hôtel de Lille ★★ (7th) : 450 F 64
Hôtel Saint-Dominique ★★ (7th) : 450 F 74
Hôtel Wallace ★★★ (15th) ❀ : 450 F 77
Hôtel Excelsior ★★ (17th) ❀ : 450 F 141
Iris Hôtel ★★ (11th) ❀ : 450 F 147
Hôtel Bastille-Spéria ★★★ (4th) : 460 F 130

from 500 to 600 F

from 600 to 700 F

Hôtel Belle Epoque ★★★ (12th) ✿ : 650 F 135
Hôtel des Deux Iles ★★★ (4th) : 650 F 7
Hôtel Sainte-Beuve ★★★ (6th) : 650 F 35
Hôtel Le Saint-Grégoire ★★★ (6th) : 650 F 37
Hôtel de Fleurie ★★★ (6th) : 650 F 51
Hôtel Etoile-Péreire ★★★ (17th) : 650 F 84
Hôtel Tilsitt-Etoile ★★★ (17th) : 650 F 93
Hôtel de Lutèce ★★★ (4th) : 660 F 8
Hôtel de la Tour d'Auvergne ★★★ (9th) : 660 F 139
Résidence Lord Byron ★★★ (8th) ✿ : 670 F 96
Hôtel Sénateur ★★★ (6th) : 680 F 47
Hôtel Franklin-Roosevelt ★★★ (8th) : 680 F 105
Hôtel de l'Abbaye St-Germain ★★★ (6th) ✿ : 690 F 40
Hôtel du Pas-de-Calais ★★★ (6th) ✿ : 690 F 57
Les Jardins d'Eiffel ★★★ (7th) ✿ : 690 F 72
Hôtel des Tuileries ★★★ (1st) : 690 F 114

from 700 to 900 F

Hôtel du Jeu de Paume ★★★★ (4th) ✿ : 700 F 6
Hôtel des Grands Hommes ★★★ (5th) : 700 F 16
Hôtel du Panthéon ★★★ (5th) : 700 F 17
Hôtel Saint-Germain-des-Prés ★★★ (6th) : 700 F 50
Hôtel Bradford ★★★ (8th) : 700 F 101
Hôtel Lido ★★★ (8th) : 700 F 108
Hôtel Gaillon-Opéra ★★★ (2nd) : 700 F 111
Hôtel de Noailles ★★★ (2nd) ✿ : 710 F 110
Hôtel de Bourgogne et Montana ★★★ (7th) : 720 F 69
Hôtel Frémiet ★★★ (16th) : 725 F 78
Hôtel Observatoire-Luxembourg ★★★ (5th) : 770 F 39
Hôtel Duminy-Vendôme ★★★ (1st) : 780 F 115
Hôtel Latitudes Saint-Germain ★★★ (6th) : 840 F 48
Left Bank Hôtel ★★★ (6th) : 850 F 11
Hôtel d'Angleterre ★★★ (6th) ✿ : 850 F 55
Hôtel Madison ★★★ (6th) : 890 F 56

more than 900 F

Hôtel Quatre Saisons - Bastille ★★★ (12th) : 900 F 134
Hôtel Duc de Saint-Simon ★★★ (7th) : 900 F 66
Terrass Hôtel ★★★★ (18th) ✿ : 900 F 145
Hôtel Alexander ★★★★ (16th) : 925 F 89
Hôtel Atala ★★★★ (8th) ✿ : 950 F 95
Hôtel Le Colbert ★★★ (5th) : 955 F 3
Hôtel Centre-Ville Etoile ★★★ (17th) : 1 000 F 91
Hôtel Centre-Ville Matignon ★★★ (8th) : 1 000 F 100
Pavillon de la Reine ★★★★ (3rd) : 1 080 F 133
Hôtel Relais Christine ★★★★ (6th) ✿ : 1 200 F 10
Relais Saint-Germain ★★★ (6th) : 1 320 F 44
Hôtel de Castille ★★★★ (1th) ✿ : 1 450 F 112
Hôtel Raphaël Paris ★★★★ L (16th) : 1 500 F 87
Hôtel Montalembert ★★★★ (7th) : 1 550 F 61
St. James's Club ★★★★ L (16th) ✿ : 1 600 F 80
La Villa Maillot ★★★★ (16th) : 1 600 F 81
Hôtel Vernet ★★★★ (8th) : 1 600 F 99
Hôtel Balzac ★★★★ (8th) : 1 680 F 97
Hôtel de Vigny ★★★★ (8th) : 1 700 F 98
Hôtel San Régis ★★★★ (8th) : 1 850 F 104

Hotels in outlying districts
Price index

Printing in Italy by Rotalfoto • Fizzonasco

Colors Separation : Graphique Productions

Chambery – France